Public Employment Labor Relations:

An Overview of Eleven Nations

Comparative Studies in Public Employment Labor Relations

Public Employment Labor Relations:

An Overview of Eleven Nations

Charles M. Rehmus, *editor*

Ann Arbor
Institute of Labor and Industrial Relations
The University of Michigan/Wayne State University
1975

This monograph is one of a series prepared under the direction of Professors Charles M. Rehmus and Russell A. Smith of The University of Michigan, and is a part of their comparative international study of labor relations in public employment. The earlier monographs in this series are:

Collective Bargaining by Public Employee Unions in Canada: Five Models, H. W. Arthurs
Public Employee Unionism in Belgium, Roger Blanpain
Public Employment Compulsory Arbitration in Australia, Gerald E. Caiden
Public Employee Labor Relations in Japan: Three Aspects, Alice H. Cook, Solomon B. Levine, and Tadashi Mitsufuji
Public Employee Trade Unionism in the United Kingdom: The Legal Framework, B. A. Hepple and Paul O'Higgins
Collective Bargaining Rights of State Officials in Sweden, Stig Jägerskiöld
Public Employee Unionism in Israel, Jerome Lefkowitz
Collective Bargaining by British Local Authority Employees, Harold M. Levinson
Collective Bargaining by Public Employees in Sweden, Harold M. Levinson
Collective Bargaining by National Employees in the United Kingdom, Raymond Loveridge
Public Employee Relations in West Germany, William H. McPherson
The State and Government Employee Unions in France, Frederic Meyers

Public Employment Labor Relations: An Overview of Eleven Nations
Copyright © 1975 by the Institute of Labor and Industrial Relations,
The University of Michigan—Wayne State University. All rights reserved.
Library of Congress Catalog Card Number: 74-22858
International Standard Book Number:
    0-87736-025-1 (Cloth edition)
    0-87736-026-X (Paper edition)
Printed in the United States of America

Contents

Preface

L ITTLE more than a decade ago, ferment in public employment labor relations began to spread rapidly throughout the
United States. Public employees at all levels of government—federal, state, municipal, and educational—began to press strongly
for the right to organize and bargain collectively over their
terms and conditions of work. In response to these pressures,
various jurisdictions of government in the United States began
to experiment with new statutory structures and administrative
procedures designed to accommodate to the bargaining mechan-
ism through which public employees were voicing their desires
and aspirations. The structures and procedures that were
devised in the various governmental jurisdictions were often
created with little or no knowledge of experience and practice
elsewhere. Most particularly, policy makers in the United States
had virtually no knowledge of the legal frameworks and procedures that had evolved to accommodate to similar pressures in
many other of the industrialized democracies of the world. Aside
from a few studies on developments in Canada, Great Britain,
and Sweden, nothing was available in the English language describing how other nations had created industrial relations systems for their public employees, and this despite the fact that
these systems were often of considerable age and stability.

As a consequence of this gap in the industrial relations and
public administration literature, we began in 1968 to seek out
foreign and American scholars who would write monographs de-

scribing and analyzing the legal framework covering public employment in other nations and the collective bargaining systems and practices that had evolved thereunder. Our efforts to bring these developments in other nations to the attention of scholars and practitioners everywhere resulted in the monograph series, *Comparative Studies in Public Employment Labor Relations.* Thus far, twelve monographs covering experience in nine nations have been published by the Institute of Labor and Industrial Relations of The University of Michigan-Wayne State University.

The continuing interest in comparative public employment labor relations was evidenced by the fact that the subject was one of the five major issue areas that were discussed during the Third World Congress of the International Industrial Relations Association held in London, England, during September of 1973. Seven of the eight studies in this volume are presentations on current legal and collective bargaining developments in public employment, original versions of which were prepared for delivery during that Congress. The study concerning similar developments in the four Nordic nations—Norway, Denmark, Sweden, and Finland—was written specifically for this volume. Five of the eight studies published here, except for those covering Austria, the United States, and the Nordic countries, concern national systems that have already been the subjects of earlier monographs in this series. All were written by different scholars than the authors of the original series, however, and bring fresh insights to each nation's experience. Moreover, these new studies often discuss facets of the subject matter area not covered in earlier monographs or describe more recent developments which will undoubtedly be of interest to those concerned with the subject.

The order in which the studies are presented here is based on the attempt to group national systems containing common elements. The two North American systems, Canada and the United States, have many similarities, not the least of which is the fact that both are federal systems in which employees at the national level bargain under rules that are quite different from those covering employees of many of the respective provinces and states. The differences, however, are equally striking. Canada has in general led its neighbor to the south in a number of areas, particularly that of experimenting with a broader right of public employees to strike. The study dealing with the Japanese system is presented next. Even though that country's public sector labor relations have many features that are unique and decidedly distinctive from those of the two North American nations, it will nevertheless be seen that Japanese labor laws do have many similarities with those of the United States.

Moving to the European nations, the system of public employee labor relations in the United Kingdom shares a common law heritage with North America, yet the largely non-statutory basis of labor relations in the United Kingdom is carried over to its public sector. The system of labor relations covering public employment in France is quite its own, sharing important elements with the French private sector. Labor relations in the public sector in France appear to be moving toward a system of continuous consultation and negotiation, a characteristic more in common with some relationships in Great Britain than with either the United States or Canada.

The systems of public employee labor relations in Germany and Austria are similar. Nevertheless, the paper on Austria presented here points to a number of significant, even striking, differences between the public sector systems in these two nations. The last study in this volume is a notable effort to compare in a short paper the similarities and differences in public employment labor relations in the four Nordic countries. Each of these systems is more like the other three than like any other nation's. Yet significant differences in laws, practices, and experience exist among the Nordic countries. Equally interesting in several respects the four Nordic systems also share elements in common with both the Germanic and the common law systems.

Three of the studies in this volume—those by Professors Kruger, Rehmus, and Verdier—were published in the Winter and Spring of 1974 by the *International Labour Review*. The Institute acknowledges with gratitude the permission received from the *Review* to republish these studies, as well as the fact that the English translation of Professor Verdier's paper was prepared by the International Labour Office. Charles Rehmus, who undertook the responsibility for bringing this volume together, wishes personally to thank Joyce Kornbluh and Doris McLaughlin for invaluable editorial assistance, and Gerry Saunders for patient retyping.

We believe that these brief studies of public employment labor relations in the industrialized democracies which they cover will be of value and interest to students and practitioners in the field. For those who desire more information, we hope this study will be read in conjunction with the parallel studies in this series that have already been published. Finally, we wish to apologize for any errors of interpretation that may have crept into it as a result of the translation and editing processes. The attempt to make one nation's legal and bargaining system intelligible to a reader who lives under a wholly different system, and who occasionally gives quite a different meaning to an identical word used by another, is a difficult one. Despite such problems, comparative studies have an important value. They give us all the opportunity to profit from the experiences—both good and bad—of others who have dealt with similar problems. Moreover, from a longer-range point of view, they demonstrate the degree to which convergence of industrial relations systems appears gradually to be taking place throughout the democratic world.

Ann Arbor, Michigan CHARLES M. REHMUS
April, 1974 RUSSELL A. SMITH

Public Employment Labor Relations:

An Overview of Eleven Nations

1
Bargaining
in the Public Sector:
Some Canadian Experiments

Arthur Kruger*

STUDENTS of industrial relations often view Canada as the fifty-first state of the United States and assume that U.S. practices prevail above the forty-ninth parallel. In many respects this generalization is accurate, particularly as it applies to industrial relations in the private sector. Although there are some notable differences between the two countries in the private sector, the similarities far outweigh the differences. In the mining and manufacturing sectors, many of the employing firms are branch plants of U.S. multinational corporations and most organized workers in Canada belong to U.S.-based international unions. Labour Legislation in Canada is closely modelled on the Wagner and Taft–Hartley Acts. Collective bargaining legislation is administered by boards that decide on the certification of an exclusive bargaining agent in the appropriate unit after ascertaining the view of the majority of workers involved. The parties are enjoined to bargain in good faith and are permitted to strike or lockout if agreements cannot be reached. Written agreements

*Professor of Political Science, University of Toronto.

3

are signed and binding. Disputes over interpretation are resolved by arbitration.

Many municipal employees in both countries are subject to arrangements similar to those applicable to the private sector. The similarity in approaches does *not* extend to public servants at the more senior levels of government. Here Canada has recently followed an independent course and experimented with a number of procedures that are unique.

Canadian federalism

Like the United States, Canada is a federal country with three levels of government. In addition to the national government centered in Ottawa, there are ten provinces, two territories, and a multitude of municipalities.

Most municipal employees are governed by the labour legislation applicable to the private sector and in some provinces even policemen, teachers, and hospital employees have the right to strike. In other provinces most of the employees are permitted to strike, but certain groups of municipal civil servants must submit to binding arbitration because society will not tolerate a withdrawal of their services. The provincial governments have jurisdiction over the legislation governing their municipal employees.

The national and the territorial governments have spheres of power allocated by the British North American Act, the written portion of the Canadian constitution. They share jurisdiction over labour relations and the administrative responsibility is much more decentralized than in the United States. As one would expect, each level of government has exclusive jurisdiction over labour legislation governing its own civil servants and employees of government-created crown corporations, agencies, and boards.

This paper will describe and evaluate industrial relations systems employed at the national level and in a few provinces that have experimented with new approaches. It will not treat municipal labour relations at any length since, as has already been indicated, the private sector model tends to apply to most of these employees.

The federal government's approach

Employees in most nationalized corporations (crown corporations) are treated in the same way as employees in the private sector who are subject to the jurisdiction of the federal government. This includes employees of a large railroad, the largest broadcasting network in Canada, the Polymer Corporation, and the major airline. All come under the Industrial Relations Disputes Investigation Act (IRDIA), belong to unions of their choice and, in most cases, are in unions that also include workers in the private sector. These employees are free to strike and have on occasion engaged in strike action. In a few cases involving strikes in the railways (including the privately owned railway), special ad hoc legislation was passed after the strikes were under way, ending the stoppages and imposing binding arbitration. In most instances, disputes have been resolved in much the same manner as they would be in the private sector.

The Public Service Staff Relations Act (PSSRA) governs employer-employee relations between the state and most of its organized civil servants as well as employees of a small number of boards and commissions. This act was proclaimed in 1967, and applies to all employees of the federal service except those in agencies under the IRDIA and members of the armed forces and the Royal Canadian Mounted Police. The latter two groups have no collective bargaining rights.

The PSSRA covers over 200,000 employees, including most of the civil servants employed under the jurisdiction of the Treasury Board. However, it also covers workers in the following eight agencies: The Atomic Energy Control Board, The Centennial Commission, The Defense Research Board, The Economic Council of Canada, The Fisheries Research Board, The National Film Board, The National Research Council, and the Northern Canada Power Commission. Workers covered by the PSSRA are scattered among 75 departments and agencies across Canada and some of them work overseas. They cover a wide range of occupations from unskilled labour to highly skilled research scientists, lawyers, and physicians. The bargaining units are unusual since they include a very large group of professionals. In addition to those indicated earlier, confidential and managerial employees are excluded from the legislation. The definition of confidential and managerial in the federal legislation is quite narrow and many supervisory employees and workers who might be considered managerial under legislation covering the private sector are permitted to organize and engage in collective bargaining. They are even permitted to belong to the same union as those whom they manage and, in some cases, they can be included in the same bargaining unit as those they manage. Only about 3 percent of federal civil servants are excluded from collective bargaining because they hold managerial or confidential jobs.

Almost all eligible employees have elected to engage in collective bargaining and have joined together in certified bargaining units. The legislation is administered by the Public Service Staff Relations Board, which has been established specifically to deal with the collective bargaining arrangements in the federal civil service. The board is tripartite in nature and has many of the functions found in labour relations boards covering employees in the private sector. Thus, for example, the board will decide on the appropriate bargaining unit, will conduct certification proceedings, will certify the bargaining unit, and will hear questions of alleged unfair labour practices. As we will see later, the board also has other functions that are not normally carried on by labour relations boards covering private employees. The chairman of the board is a permanent appointee of the government who is acceptable to all concerned. In addition to the chairman, there is a panel nominated by the various major unions engaged in bargaining with the government and a panel of employer nominees. All cases that go before the board are heard by a tripartite panel, which includes equal numbers of union and employer representatives.

The government has also established other machinery to carry out this legislation. The Pay Research Bureau of the federal government, which operates under the Public Service Staff Relations Board, is an independent agency that gathers statistical data on wage developments outside the federal public service to assist the parties in collective bargaining and the arbitration tribunals discussed below. The Pay Research Bureau operates with advice from unions and employers.

There is also a tripartite arbitration tribunal established to hear interest disputes. The tribunal has several permanent chairmen who are acceptable to all parties. In addition it has a panel of employer nominees and a panel of employee nominees. Each arbitration case is heard by a three-man panel consisting of the chairman plus a nominee from each of the panels. The decisions of the tribunal, however, are the decisions of the chairman.

The government also appoints an adjudicator to handle grievance disputes under the collective agreements. The work of a chief adjudicator who is acceptable to all parties is supplemented by the efforts of other adjudicators who assist him. The grievance machinery is open to those who are eligible to engage in collective bargaining and to other employees who either choose not to bargain or who are ineligible for collective bargaining.

Scope of bargaining

The legislation differs significantly from the private sector in defining the scope of collective bargaining. Matters that are specifically precluded from collective bargaining include:

(1) Anything that requires action by Parliament, except for the granting of money to carry out the collective agreements;

(2) Matters covered by the following legislation: the Government Employees Compensation Act, the Government Vessel Discipline Act, the Public Service Employment Act, and the Public Service Superannuation Act.

These pieces of legislation are designed primarily to protect the merit principle of appointment, transfer, and promotion, which are excluded from collective bargaining. They also cover matters such as superannuation, death benefits, and accident compensation, which are also outside the scope of bargaining. These is-sues are open for discussion by the parties through the National Joint Council composed of representatives of the government and most of the major associations engaged in bargaining with the government. The government also exercises unilateral con-trol over the classification system and job assignments.

Choice of routes

Under the federal legislation the bargaining agent has the op-tion of choosing between two possible routes for resolving those disputes that cannot be resolved through negotiation: (1) to submit the dispute to a conciliation board (if the board fails to resolve the dispute, the bargaining agent is then free to engage in a strike) ; (2) to submit the dispute to arbitration, with con-ciliation by a conciliation officer as a possibility prior to arbitra-tion. This decision is entirely in the hands of the bargaining agent. Under the legislation the government is bound to accept the bargaining agent's decision as to the route chosen, thus providing the bargaining agent with a very powerful weapon in collective bargaining. Groups that are unwilling or unable to en-gage in effective strike action can compel the government to sub-mit disputes to compulsory arbitration. Other groups that may find the strike an effective weapon can, in fact, engage in work stoppages. The bargaining agent is free to alter its choice of route from one set of contract negotiations to the other. It must, however, designate the route to be followed prior to the start of bargaining on a given contract.

As of March 31, 1973, there were 108 bargaining units oper-ating with almost 198,000 employees under the PSSRA. Of those, 89 units with 130,484 members opted for arbitration and only 19 units with 67,376 employees selected the strike option. There had been only five legal strikes up to that time.

Designated employees

Emergency services that the federal legislation defines as crucial to the "safety and security of the public," can be handled by designated employees who are not permitted to engage in strikes. The bargaining agent is entitled to information on the probable number of designated employees prior to its selection of the appropriate bargaining route. It can ask the employer to submit a list of these employees, who must carry on services should a strike occur, and the employer is required to comply with this request soon after it is received. The bargaining agent may choose to accept some or all of the designated employees. Should it decide to challenge a portion of the list of designated employees, the case is decided by the Public Service Staff Relations Board. Thus far in all those cases where the bargaining agent has requested a list of designated employees, about 13.6 percent of employees in these bargaining units have been designated. Of course, the proportions designated will vary greatly among bargaining units.

The conciliation-strike route

The following employees are forbidden from striking: (1) Those designated as indicated above; (2) Those not in a certified bargaining unit; (3) Those in a bargaining unit that has opted for the arbitration route; (4) Those in a bargaining unit covered by a collective agreement that remains in force; (5) Those in a bargaining unit that have opted for the strike route but are still subject to the conciliation process.

Those who have opted for the strike route include: (1) approximately 25,000 postal workers; (2) approximately 2,300 ship repair workers; (3) approximately 1,200 employees in printing operations; (4) 1,000 employees in air traffic control; (5) the electronic technicians employed at air terminals. Nonsupervisory postal workers have not been considered designated employees.

Arbitration

The disputes that are submitted to arbitration are subject to a variety of stipulations. The most important appears to be the following:

(1) No matter may be brought before the arbitration tribunal that has not been raised earlier in collective bargaining. All matters that are excluded by law from bargaining are, of course, not subject to arbitration.

(2) In addition, there are certain issues that are bargainable but are not subject to arbitration. Arbitration is limited under Section 70 to "rates of pay, hours of work, leave entitlement, standards of discipline, and other terms and conditions of employment directly related thereto." Under Section 56, Arbitration Tribunals cannot deal with matters that require action by Parliament except for the expenditure of funds. Arbitration under Section 70 specifically cannot deal with the merit principle of appointment, assignment, lay-off, or release, nor can it deal with matters involving workers not in the bargaining unit. Thus, for example, while the parties are free to deal with a matter such as union security through negotiations, under Section 70 the Arbitration Board cannot deal with such a matter should the parties fail to resolve it during the process of bargaining.

The postal strikes

Because of the recent experience with public service strikes in many other countries, there is great interest in Canadian strikes in the federal service. In Canada we have already had four postal strikes. Although the first was illegal, the others were legal because they came after the Public Service Staff Relations Act was passed. In all cases the strikes lasted for some time and the public suffered considerable inconvenience. There have also been two strikes that severely disrupted air traffic for a period of time. However, in all cases, a settlement was ultimately reached and the nation managed to survive without these services.

Problems of the federal act

The most significant problems experienced under the federal legislation appear to be:

(1) Fragmentation of the bargaining units: The certification procedures followed under the act have resulted in a large num-

ber of bargaining units in the federal public service. Although some fragmentation was necessary and desirable, given the enormous size and diversity of employment in the public service, the degree of fragmentation has probably been excessive. It leaves many of the bargaining units too weak to find the strike option a really effective one. Strikes could occur in many of these bargaining units for considerable periods of time with little pressure on the employer for any kind of settlement. It also opens the question of "whipsawing" by the bargaining agents as they use either the strike or arbitration process to secure a gain for one group of employees, which they then attempt to spread to other groups of employees. Finally it means that too many issues are constantly being negotiated. The employer is bargaining simultaneously with various bargaining agents and some of the larger associations that bargain for a sizable number of bargaining units are also constantly engaged in collective bargaining with the same employer. In each of these bargaining sessions the same issues come up repeatedly, particularly in the areas of fringe benefits and working conditions. Too often the parties are bargaining with an eye to setting precedents for other groups, and the arbitrators must be conscious of the implications of their decision in a given case for other groups of employees. If arbitrators take this consideration too seriously, they may refuse to innovate in the area of fringe benefit and working conditions for fear of opening up the possibility of whipsawing.

(2) Limitations on the scope of arbitration: Since the subjects that can be dealt with under arbitration are much narrower than those that can be handled through the collective bargaining process, the bargaining agents often find that the employer can use the threat of forcing arbitration in order to compel the bargaining agents to agree. Thus the employer may indicate his willingness to make concessions on certain matters not subject to arbitration only if the bargaining agent foregoes arbitration. Otherwise, the employer may refuse to concede these matters and, in effect, impose arbitration. The bargaining agent will find that the arbitration tribunal is precluded from discussing some of the important issues.

The provinces

The provinces have tended to copy the federal government in legislation applicable to labour relations in the private sector. However, only New Brunswick has adopted the federal model in the public sector. This section of the paper will concentrate on a few provinces where significant experiments are under way.

New Brunswick

New Brunswick is the only province to adopt the federal model thus far. However, the New Brunswick approach deviates from the federal legislation in a number of ways related to the choice between the strike and arbitration. In New Brunswick, both parties are free to *propose* arbitration as an alternative to the strike, whereas in the federal model only the union has this prerogative. Furthermore, during the course of bargaining the parties can alter their preferences between the two options. Arbitration cannot be imposed unless both parties agree. If either party rejects this alternative, a stoppage is the only available alternative.

Prior to a strike, the union must secure the support of a majority of those taking part in a strike vote. If a stoppage occurs, the union does not picket, and the government in return agrees not to attempt to operate the struck facilities until the dispute is resolved.

New Brunswick's legislation applies not only to its civil servants and employees in crown agencies but also to school teachers and hospital employees who are under special legislation in most other provinces.

Ontario

With the exception of liquor store workers, the provincial police, and a few other groups, Ontario civil service employees are all organized in a single large association. The Civil Service Association of Ontario (CSAO) bargains on behalf of some 43,000 members. While strikes are illegal in public employment, the parties have agreed to submit unresolved interest disputes to a tripartite arbitration tribunal. The arbitration tribunal's awards are final and binding insofar as the provincial government has always agreed to implement them. There is no reason to expect that the province would deviate from past practices.

The pattern of bargaining is based on the fact that there is one union for all the employees involved. In contrast to the federal system and the private sector, wages are decided separately from fringe benefits and working conditions, which are set for the entire service in negotiations involving smaller groups of employees in related occupations.

Saskatchewan

By legislation enacted in 1944, Saskatchewan was the first jurisdiction in Canada to sanction civil service strikes. Public employees, including hospital employees and policemen, are covered by the legislation applicable to the private sector. However, this approach does not cover teachers and fire fighters who are subject to compulsory arbitration if agreement is not reached.

Quebec

The government of Quebec models bargaining in the public sector on the private sector model and rejects arbitration as inappropriate since it places undue power to determine the level of public expenditures in the hands of nonelected arbitrators. All employees, including hospital employees, teachers, civil servants, and crown agency workers, may strike if agreement cannot be reached in negotiations. However, policemen, other peace officers, and firemen are subject to compulsory arbitration.

To protect the public interest, the government copied the U.S. Taft–Hartley Act and provided for an 80-day injunction in cases of strikes endangering "the public health and safety." This can only delay a strike for an 80-day period after which no further delay can be imposed on strike activity. Furthermore, civil servants cannot strike until the parties agree on the methods of maintaining essential services during a stoppage. If the parties fail to agree on the definition of essential services or the manner of maintaining them, these issues are to be decided by the Labour Court.

In 1972, the civil servants, school teachers and hospital workers all struck in a united front after they failed to negotiate an
agreement with the government. The provisions of the act concerning the maintenance of essential services were ignored and
an injunction issued by the courts also failed to end the strikes.
Only a special ad hoc law with strong penalties for violation
managed to force the workers to return to their jobs while bargaining was resumed.

Some conclusions

One hesitates to draw any firm conclusions based on the limited
Canadian experience with collective bargaining for public servants. Only the Saskatchewan Act has been in force for a long
enough period to clearly discern some trends. The other acts described here have all operated for less than a decade. Nonethe-
less, some inferences can be drawn, albeit with varying degrees
of confidence.

Management

In every jurisdiction, bargaining policy is closely controlled by
the cabinet, usually through the treasury board. Departments of
labour play no role other than to provide conciliation services.
In the federal system, even the conciliation function is handled
by a special independent board. Those conducting collective
bargaining on behalf of the government are often recruited
from the private sector. Government involvement has grown so
rapidly that there was no choice but to involve those with experience outside the public service.

Labour

Freedom of association exists across Canada. However, the form
of permissible association and the relationship of employee organizations with the state varies greatly among jurisdictions. In
some provinces, the government has severely restricted the number of organizations it recognizes and negotiates with. In Ontario, for example, the statute effectively accords recognition

rights for all civil servants to one union and the employer refuses to bargain with separate organizations for dissident groups of employees. In other instances, provision is made for certification and recognition of bargaining agents covering distinct subgroups of public servants such as engineers, lighthousekeepers, and other employees. The federal system with over 100 separate bargaining units is an example.

Most organized civil servants belong to unions composed primarily of public servants, although at all three levels of government there are examples of groups affiliated with private sector employees. Workers in crown agencies are divided between public service unions and unions that also include private sector employees. Most railway and airline workers in the crown-owned firms are in unions not limited to the public sector. On the other hand, many utility workers belong to organizations that are predominantly composed of public service employees. A number of public service unions are affiliated at the provincial and national levels with union federations involving both public and private sector unions.

In the future some of the blue-collar workers in public employment may join powerful private sector unions organizing in their occupations. There is evidence in Ontario that some highway and hospital employees would prefer affiliation with unions such as the Teamsters. Similarly, public service unions may extend their interest to other groups. In Ontario, the CSAO has moved to organize workers in community colleges and universities. Some of the professional unions may also decide to extend their activities to the private sector, which remains largely unorganized.

Collective bargaining

Canadian employees in municipal service and in government-owned enterprises have long enjoyed collective bargaining rights. Until recently, civil servants were denied bargaining and, at most, had consultation arrangements. Since the mid-sixties, the senior levels of government have become more receptive to collective bargaining, and Canada has gone much further than the United States in accepting either arbitration on the one hand or strikes on the other as the ultimate method of resolving disputes.

The experience with arbitration

Thus far, in those areas subject to compulsory arbitration, the parties appear to be reasonably content with the process and its results. There are, of course, exceptions to this generalization and periodic complaints. The most vociferous opponents of the system are hospital employees who blame the process for their low-paid status.

The greatest weakness in the process is its limited ability to cope with working conditions. With the proliferation of bargaining units in the federal system, arbitrators are reluctant to set precedents that could spread to other groups with unforeseen consequences. Furthermore, the arbitrators change from one dispute to another and have neither the knowledge nor the time to learn what is often at stake in a request to alter a working rule.

The Ontario system avoids these problems by system-wide bargaining on working conditions and employing a permanent chairman of the arbitration board who has accumulated expertise. However, these gains are balanced by an inability to effect a trade-off between wage increases, altered working conditions, and fringe benefits since these three areas are covered in separate negotiation. Furthermore, the compulsion to organize in a single bargaining unit has left some disaffected groups of civil servants with no option but to remain in a union that they do not support. Finally, with system-wide bargaining on working conditions, only changes that are desirable on a system-wide basis tend to be considered seriously, and demands that are meaningful only to small groups of employees are likely to be ignored.

The experience with strikes

Canadian experience with strikes as a legally sanctioned option has been limited. However, some things are now obvious. The government is bound to arrange matters so that no strike that brings the government or any significant part of it to a halt will be tolerated for long. In the federal system, legislation provides means to hand the fragmentation of bargaining units and the prohibition of strikes for "designated employees" and ensures that strikes are socially and politically tolerable. The Quebec government undoubtedly will act to insure that a repetition of the 1972 strikes will never recur.

Since strikes of public servants cause no economic harm to the state, the union can only impose its will by winning over public support. Low-paid postal workers successfully used this weapon, whereas the more highly paid air traffic controllers merely annoyed the public and might have achieved more by arbitration.

In the federal system, where strikes and arbitration are alternatives for some groups, the government appears determined to induce unions to select arbitration. To achieve this, government policy is to resist strike settlements that appear more generous than settlements obtained by comparable groups through arbitration. This policy appears to be working since only a small number of bargaining units have opted to strike.

Inflation, guidelines, and collective bargaining

Once governments engage in bargaining, they soon find themselves the pattern setters for many categories of labour because they are large, very visible employers, and press coverage of settlements in the public sector is usually very thorough. Governments are under considerable pressure from the private sector to resist innovations or large settlements that could spread to the private sector.

With strong inflationary pressures, the Canadian government in recent years has on occasion proclaimed guidelines for permissible wage settlements. This tended to create a focus on settlements in the public sector where leadership in restraint was to be expected. The government was compelled to adopt a rigid stance in collective bargaining and refused to exceed its own guidelines. The arbitration process produced some settlements in excess of the guidelines, but arbitrators soon appeared to adopt the guidelines as a major criterion in their decisions.

Unions in the public sector were concerned that they were compelled to behave in the socially acceptable manner, whereas settlements in the private sector continued to exceed the guidelines. If governments do not face the cost restraint operating in the private sector, they do act under pressure to restrain tax increases and to provide a model for all in the battle against inflation. Our experience indicates that these pressures can be as strong as competitive market forces in stiffening employer opposition to union demands.

The extent of the public sector

The size and range of public sector activities are constantly expanding, and the growth potential is particularly strong at the provincial level. Education and health services are now financed largely by the provinces, and concern with cost of these services is mounting. Some provinces have already assumed direct responsibility for bargaining with the employees in these sectors; other jurisdictions are likely to be pushed in the same direction. This will introduce collective bargaining for groups formerly hostile to unions: doctors, dentists, pharmacists, and professors. Working out suitable arrangements for these groups is likely to be difficult. In addition, concern with the environment and with other problems involving regional planning creates pressures for a shift of functions from local governments to the provincial governments, which often results in a change in unions and in bargaining procedures.

Governments are likely to find themselves faced with no acceptable alternative for dispute resolution. If unions are permitted to strike, they will seek ways of conducting effective strikes that governments are unlikely to tolerate. On the other hand, one wonders how long governments will be prepared to permit arbitrators to formulate major areas of economic policy, namely the cost of public services and the pattern of wage settlements.

2

Labor Relations in the Public Sector in the United States

Charles M. Rehmus *

P UBLIC service is the most rapidly growing major sector of
employment in the United States. In the last 30 years, public
employment has tripled, growing from 4.2 million to 13.1 million employees. Today, nearly one out of five workers in the
United States is on a government payroll.

Part of this dramatic increase in public employment can be attributed to population growth, necessitating a proportional increase in publicly provided services. More fundamental to
growth than simple demographic change, however, have been
increases in the demand for new services, shifts from private to
public provision of certain kinds of service, and advances in
technology that have intensified the need for new levels of existing public services. Ever since the Great Depression of the
1930s, U.S. citizens have expected government to provide more
and more service for more and more people, and the provision
of these services has created many new public jobs. Education,

*Co-Director, Institute of Labor and Industrial Relations, The University of
Michigan-Wayne State University.

19

health care, the public highway system, and police and fire protection are the largest sources of employment at state and local levels of government and at the federal level, more jobs have been created by the government's expanding role in the international arena.

This growth of government service has not been steady or equal at all levels of government in the U.S. federal system. Any consideration of public employment and of public employee labor relations must distinguish between three primary levels of government—federal, state, and local—as well as the large postal and educational subsections of federal and local government. Each level of government has specific areas of administrative authority and service responsibility, which are in turn affected by specific constituency demands and its own laws regulating public employer-employee labor relations.

Federal government.   Federal government employment has increased the least of the three primary levels of government, expanding by only 40 percent between 1950 and 1970. This represents a decline in the federal proporation of all public employment from 33 to 23 percent during the same period. It should be noted that the federal government's share of total government expenditures has not declined proportionately because nearly half of all federal expenditures go into national defense. If defense expenditures were discounted, the federal expenditure share would be approximately the same as the federal employment share, about 23 percent. In the United States, the federal government's income is derived primarily from individual and corporate income taxes and, in addition to defense and military expenditures, is spent on social welfare insurance, veterans' benefits, agricultural and natural resources programs, international gifts and loans, space research, and a multitude of general welfare programs.

State government.   State employment represents 27 percent of total government employment in the United States. State governments derive their income primarily from sales and excise taxes and, increasingly, from individual and corporate income taxes. Primary state expenditures go to maintain and administer public education, highways and waterways, and public welfare and health programs.

Local government. Local government accounts for 50 percent of all public employment in the United States. Local governments derive their income primarily from taxes on real property and from subventions out of state and federal revenue-sharing funds. They carry out the police, public safety, and sanitation functions and, more recently, have been expending a large share of the monies that are devoted to urban renewal programs.

Education. Education ranks second only to national defense in terms of public economic expenditures in the United States. Twenty-nine percent of all government expenditures are directed to national defense and related purposes, and approximately 16 percent goes to education. Education accounts for 32 percent of all public employment and represents slightly over half of all state and local employment. Although state governments bear the responsibility for establishing and maintaining the public school system, the actual operation of the schools is ordinarily delegated to local school districts. Over 90 percent of all local school districts are administratively independent of any other local governmental unit. Moreover, most school disticts are atypical in the U.S. governmental structures in that their local governing bodies—school boards or the equivalent—have both executive and legislative authority. School boards make as well as administer educational policy, and most school boards have been given the authority to levy property taxes, subject to voter approval.

Postal service. The fifth substantial sector of public employment in the United States is unusual: The U.S. Postal Service is by far the largest and only major public corporation in the United States. Until 1970, the Post Office Department had been one of the component agencies of the federal government. Its employees were federal civil servants whose conditions of employment were legislated by the U.S. Congress. Its work force was also unusual, having been overwhelmingly union-organized since the 19th century, and restless as well as militant. An unprecedented major strike by postal workers, which began on the eastern seaboard and extended to many other parts of the nation, created pressure for the immediate realization of a long-discussed idea, the transformation of the Post Office Department into a public corporation. In general, postal service employees are now subject to the labor relations rules and regulations that pertain in the private sector. The main remnant of postal employees' former civil servant status is the retention of the ban on their right to strike in the event of bargaining impasses, and the substitution of compulsory binding arbitration.

This notable modification in the status of postal employment is only one of many fundamental changes in the U.S. public service in the United States during the 1960s—a period that has been called "the decade of the public employee revolution."

Background of public employee labor relations

Workers in the industrial private sector in the United States were given the statutory right to organize and bargain collectively in the 1930s. By 1960, approximately 30 percent of all nonagricultural private sector employees were represented by unions. Yet by this same date there was practically no unionization in the public sector other than in the traditionally-organized postal service and in a few other isolated situations.

The reasons for this delay are complex. In part they stem from certain philosophical ideas long prevalent in the nation. Traditional concepts of sovereignty asserted that government is and should be supreme, hence immune from contravening forces and pressures such as collective bargaining. Related to this concept was that of the illegality of delegation of sovereign power. This asserted that public decision making could only be done by elected or appointed public officials whose unilateral and complete discretion was unchallengeable.

More practical considerations also delayed the advent of public employee unionism in the United States. The private sector unions and their federations were fully occupied in trying to organize in the private sector, and they had neither the money nor the energy to turn to the public sector until the 1960s. Equally or more important, public employees were not generally dissatisfied with their terms and conditions of employment and, except in isolated cases, did not press for collective bargaining rights. Although the wages and salaries of public employees in the United States had traditionally lagged slightly behind comparable private sector salaries, the greater fringe benefits and job security associated with public employment were usually thought to be adequate compensation.

By the late 1950s and early 1960s, several of these practical considerations, which had delayed public employee unionism, had disappeared. Moreover, new factors came into play that produced a new militancy although their sequence or relative importance is difficult to assess. Change increasingly became endemic in American society as more and more groups, including public employees, found it commonplace to challenge the established order. Some public employees were made less secure by organizational and technological changes as government came under pressure to reduce the rate of tax increases and therefore sought ways to increase efficiency and lower unit labor costs. Public employee wages and salaries began to lag further behind those in the unionized private sector as the post-war inflationary spiral continued. The private sector unions saw the large and growing employment in the nonunion public sector as a fertile alternative field of recruitment that might compensate for their failure after 1956 to increase membership steadily in the private sector. Finally, many observers of public employment both in and out of government began strongly and publicly to question the logic by which government protected collective bargaining in the private sector while refusing to grant similar privileges and protections in the public sector.

By the 1960s these practical challenges to the traditional arguments of sovereignty and illegal delegation of powers had gained momentum in a number of government jurisdictions. The city of New York, the school board of that same city, and the state of Wisconsin gave modified collective bargaining rights to their public employees. Most importantly, in 1962, an executive order by President Kennedy gave federal employees a limited version of the rights that private employees had received 30 years before. These seminal breakthroughs led increasingly to similar kinds of state legislation, particularly in the more industrialized states. Today over 30 states have granted some form of collective bargaining rights to some or all of their public employees. President Nixon in two executive orders expanded and clarified the bargaining rights of federal employees. Fifty-five percent of civilian federal employees are now represented for collective bargaining purposes, and this figure excludes the traditionally organized postal service. Although precise figures are not available, probably one-third of all state, municipal, and educational employees are similarly represented and this fraction is growing steadily.

As a matter of general law in the United States, the federal courts have held that an individual's right to form and join a union is a protected right under the First Amendment to the Constitution. Federal courts have also held, however, that there is no constitutional right to bargain collectively in either the public or the private sector. As far as the public sector is concerned, only a statute or an executive order can force an employer to bargain collectively. Recent state court decisions suggest that their public authorities are under no legally enforceable duty to bargain in the absence of a statutory requirement, but that they are free to do so if they choose. In short, public and private employees in the United States have the constitutional right to form and join unions and to attempt to gain collective bargaining rights. But their employers, even today, are under no legal obligation to bargain collectively unless this duty is imposed upon them.

The reticence of about 20 of the states to allow collective bargaining in the public sector is largely based on the fear of increased strike action. In reality, however, many public employee strikes have taken place in jurisdictions where collective bargaining was regarded as unlawful, and demands for recognition and bargaining rights constitute the second highest cause of strikes in the public sector. Many public employee strikes could have been averted had the employer been required by statute to recognize and bargain with the employee organization. Furthermore, the acceptance of collective bargaining in the public sector does not necessarily call for the acceptance of strikes in support of bargaining demands. Experience in various jurisdictions of U.S. government shows that the issues of public employee bargaining and public employee strikes are quite separate and distinct. This subject will be further discussed below.

The federal experience

As one of his first official acts in 1961, President Kennedy appointed a task force of high administration officials to review and advise him on labor-management relations in the federal service. The task force report served as the basis for Executive Order 10988 that gave all federal employees the right to join (or not to join) organizations of their choice. In effect, this original federal executive order was designed to encourage union representation throughout the federal service. It did so by means of a device unique in labor management experience in the United States, the creation of three levels of recognition. An employee organization having any members at all within a federal department or agency could be granted *informal* recognition, which gave it the right to speak to management on behalf of its members. An organization representing as many as 10 percent, but fewer than 50 percent of the employees, within an appropriate bargaining unit in the federal structure was entitled to *formal* recognition and to consult and be consulted by federal managers on personnel policies broadly affecting its members. An organization that represented a majority of employees within an appropriate bargaining unit was entitled to *exclusive* recognition, the characteristic form of union recognition in North America, which gives the right to negotiate a written bargaining agreement.

Under this original federal executive order, the scope of bargaining was limited to basic working conditions; wages and fringe benefits continued then as now to be set by Congress. Moreover, a very strong management rights clause had to be included in every federal agreement recognizing management's right to direct employees: to hire, promote, transfer, assign, suspend, demote, discharge, and discipline them; to relieve them from duty because of lack of work; and to determine the methods, means, and personnel by which operations are to be conducted.

Despite these limitations on the scope of collective bargaining, which have been retained in all subsequent executive orders, union representation expanded rapidly in the federal civilian service. Excluding the postal service, only 19,000 federal employees were in exclusive bargaining units at the end of 1962. By the end of 1972, 1,083,000 federal employees were in 3,400 exclusive units. This represented 55 percent of the federal civilian work force, which no longer included the postal service. Although approximately 200 different employee organizations represent federal employees, the major employee organizations in the federal service are of three basic kinds:

(1) Unions with all or a major proportion of their membership in the federal service. Typical of such organizations is the American Federation of Government Employees, with some 325,-000 federal members. It is an affiliate of the AFL-CIO, the large, predominantly private sector union federation. Another example is the National Federation of Federal Employees, an organization with a membership exceeding 100,000, which is independent of the AFL-CIO.

(2) Unions with a major proportion of membership in the private sector but with substantial federal membership. Typical of such organizations is the Service Employees' International Union, an AFL-CIO affiliate with nearly 450,000 members, over 30 percent of whom are in government service.

(3) Independent associations or unions whose members are often professional and limited to a specific employee craft or agency. Typical of such associations in the federal service are the National Treasury Employees Union and the Professional Air Traffic Controllers Association. The latter association has recently affiliated with a private sector AFL-CIO affiliate.

Executive Order 10988 was followed in 1969 by a second labor relations executive order issued by President Nixon. This new order, EO 11491, favored the single form of union recognition characteristic in the private sector, majority exclusive recognition. It also removed from the individual federal agencies and departments much of the authority they had retained for labor-management affairs during the seven years of EO 10988, vesting this authority instead in a coordinated federal labor relations system. Under EO 11491, the Assistant Secretary of Labor for Labor Management Relations has the authority to determine appropriate bargaining units, to supervise elections, and to rule on alleged unfair labor practices. Thus the Department of Labor now plays much the same role in the federal labor management program as does the National Labor Relations Board in the private sector. EO 11491 also broadened the scope of negotiability in several areas of working conditions. Perhaps the most important of these was permission for agencies to negotiate agreements providing for binding neutral arbitration of employee grievances. This replaced the former system wherein arbitral decisions were only advisory.

The foregoing is not intended to suggest that labor relations in the federal services are now or are becoming identical with those in the private sector. A number of obvious differences remain. Bargaining unit determinations have resulted in less fragmentation and fewer specific craft units than in the private sector. Professional employees who are prevalent in government are treated in special ways that are not characteristic of organized professionals in the private sector. The continuous reorganization of government agencies and activities brings constant changes in unit structure and federal bargaining relationships, which are far less common in private industry.

Allegations of unfair labor practices in the federal government must be processed and carried forward by the protesting unions themselves rather than by an independent government agency like the National Labor Relations Board or the equivalent. Quite unlike the private sector, the federal program still forbids "union security" clauses that require union membership or financial support from members of a bargaining unit. The federal government maintains its "no strike" ban and has taken punitive measures against employees who engage in coercive job actions. (The one significant exception to this generalization regarding punishment was the postal employees' strike. As noted previously, this strike was one of the factors leading to the creation of a new public corporation for postal services in which postal workers acquired a largely private sector status. Ironically, however, they are still under a "no strike" ban.)

In general, progress and change in federal labor management relations thus far have not been as great as the growth of unionism per se. The most important reason for this is the continuing limitation on the scope of negotiable issues. Unions of federal employees are maintaining their pressure to broaden the scope of bargaining, however, primarily through increasing the coverage and size of bargaining units. Any subject is negotiable that falls within the discretionary authority of the highest level of management directly supervising employees in the unit. As unit sizes gradually increase over time, it is believed that the scope of negotiable issues will ultimately reach practically all personnel matters that are within the discretion and control of each individual federal agency.

State and local experience

Although the federal government's power to regulate interstate commerce has been construed by the Supreme Court as giving Congress the authority to regulate relations between local governments and their employees, no federal statute has been enacted in this area. In practice this has meant that the structuring of labor-management relationships and of collective bargaining mechanisms in the states has been left to the individual states, no doubt wisely since the myriad of state and local government fiscal policies, tax structures, and budgetary and personnel practices make federal determination of labor-management policies and enforcement mechanisms for local governments virtually impossible. The result has been, however, that the individual states and municipalities have developed widely differing structures and mechanisms of labor relations. Prior to the example set by the 1962 federal executive order, only Wisconsin had enacted legislation establishing bargaining mechanisms for its public employees. Since then, 30 of the 50 states have enacted some kind of legislation concerning all or some groups of their public employees. Twenty-one have enacted comprehensive statutes in this area. A comprehensive statute is defined as one that: (1) guarantees public employees the right to bargain collectively, (2) establishes procedures for selection of employee representatives, (3) prescribes remedies for unfair labor practices committed by employers or employee organizations and, (4) provides dispute resolution mechanisms.

The coverage and scope of state statutes are extremely varied. Some states cover all state and local government employees, including teachers, under one statute. Other states have excluded state civil servants from statutes that cover all local government and educational employees. Fifteen states have enacted separate statutes covering teachers, and ten have statutes covering only firemen and/or policemen.

To determine representation rights and appropriate bargaining units in the public sector, most states use the same agencies that serve the private sector. This tends to promote a uniform approach to labor-management relationships in the two sectors. Other states have set up new and separate agencies to administer public sector labor relations, while a third group of states has left the creation of administrative and enforcement machinery to local initiative. Finally, although most importantly, the scope of collective bargaining under most state statutes is broader than that in the federal government, usually covering wages, hours, and fringe benefits, as well as working conditions.

A few examples will illustrate the variety of state experience. New York and its local units of government have over one million public employees, 90 percent of whom are now covered by collective bargaining. Some 12,000 labor agreements exist with 1,100 different units of local and municipal government throughout the state. On the other hand, several hundred thousand state civil servants have been placed in only six bargaining units on a statewide basis. The broad collective bargaining coverage has been achieved in New York despite the fact that its law has been largely effective in preventing strikes over collective bargaining impasses in all but New York City itself.

In Michigan, state civil servants have no right to bargain collectively but employees of local government and education units do. In less than ten years, over 90 percent of Michigan teachers and over one-third of all employee of counties, municipalities, and townships in the state have come to be represented for collective bargaining purposes.

The union that represents most local government employees in Michigan, as well as throughout the nation, is the American Federation of State, County, and Municipal Employees (AFSCME). AFSCME has more than doubled in size in the last ten years and has over half a million members nationally. It is potentially the largest union in the United States simply because its jurisdiction gives it an organizing potential of over eight million employees. Other unions, some with their primary base in the private sector, such as the Teamsters and the Steelworkers, are also organizing and bargaining for tens of thousands of local and municipal government employees.

Michigan, like almost all other states, has maintained its ban on public employee strikes. In practice, however, such strikes are fairly frequent, and employees engaging in them are seldom punished. In recognition of this growing *de facto* right to strike, four states have legalized strikes for some or all public employees. Hawaii and Pennsylvania have eliminated their strike bans. But even these two states have provided for special safeguards in strikes endangering the public health or safety. The one group of public employees who by general consensus cannot be allowed to strike are the uniformed public safety services—police, firefighters, deputy sheriffs, and prison guards. As an alternative to the strike for these uniformed services, eight states including Michigan, Pennsylvania, and Wisconsin are experimenting with varieties of compulsory abritration systems.

At the other extreme to states with comprehensive public employee statutes are those that have no legislation in the field, except perhaps for a blanket strike prohibition. Yet even in these states, organization of municipal employees is growing rapidly. In the major cities of Ohio, local recognition and bargaining rights are being granted as a matter of course but without statutory authority or control. Even in some southern states, where regulatory laws are least common, recognition strikes are being won by sanitation and hospital workers, and by AFSCME on behalf of many categories of municipal workers.

As a gross generalization and with important exceptions, collective bargaining for public employees at the state and municipal levels appears to be shifting authority for personnel issues to the executive branch of local government at the expense of the legislative branch and of traditional civil service systems. Civil service boards or commissions recruit, examine, train, and rate government employees and provide for their retirement. Their fundamental responsibility is to see that government employees are recruited and promoted based on merit rather than on partisan political considerations. It has recently been suggested by some commentators that some elements of these existing civil service systems seem doomed to be replaced by collective bargaining structures. In addition, authority for collective bargaining increasingly appears to be centralized within the executive branch of many cities, with primary bargaining responsibility for all departments of the city assigned to an individual or office directly responsible to the chief executive. As yet, however, multiemployer bargaining units covering more than one governmental unit are almost unknown in local government in the United States.

As a major generalization, the growth of a *de facto* right to strike in some states is creating some severe problems for their local governments. Because municipal unions are only slightly subject to the discipline of the product market and because their membership is relatively immune from the threat of technological displacement, their collective bargaining demands have often been high and inflexible. Because the services of some members of municipal unions are deemed essential, cities such as Detroit, Philadelphia, and New York have found it difficult or impossible to muster counter-pressure to employee strikes. Local bargaining impasses tend to induce a crisis atmosphere in which public decisions are often made in the hope of remedying immediate crisis situations. In some cities this has meant that carefully evaluated wage policies developed over the years have been jettisoned because garbage is piling up in the streets, buses are not running, or police officers are threatening some sort of protest action. In sum, the unions with the greatest leverage on the public appear, for the moment at least, to be advantaging themselves at the expense of other categories of public employees who work in less critical areas. In other cases these powerful groups have advantaged themselves at the expense of the level of public services provided. At this point in time, no other group of claimants on the public tax funds seems in a position to exercise the same amount of influence on public resource allocation as the powerful and cohesive municipal unions.

The experience in education

Teachers are perhaps as widely organized and are engaging in as many forms of bargaining as any group of public employees in the United States. As previously noted, some states that have not passed general statutes affecting public employees have specifically granted teachers the right to organize and bargain. Other states, such as California and Minnesota, while not granting complete collective bargaining rights to teachers, have granted them the right to "meet and confer" with local school boards. In theory, the "meet and confer" right implies that management must listen to employee suggestions but retains a more or less free hand in making decisions. Where teacher organizations are strong, however, the limited right has had results largely indistinguishable from collective bargaining. Finally, in some major cities such as Chicago and Cleveland, collective bargaining between teacher organizations and local boards of education has taken place for a number of years without specific authorization of law.

One of the main reasons for the substantial extent of organization among public school teachers has been the competition between the two major federations of teachers, the American Federation of Teachers (AFT) and the National Education Association (NEA). The AFT is affiliated with the AFL-CIO and its leadership generally feels a fairly close identity with the trade union movement. The NEA, on the other hand, is a long-time professional organization of approximately one million classroom teachers and their supervisors. In the past decade, the

NEA has given up its traditional reluctance to engage in collective bargaining and has competed aggressively for bargaining rights with the AFT. The competition between these two groups is analogous to that which existed between the AFL and the CIO during the 1930s and 40s, and just as employees in private industry probably were better served because of the competition that occurred in those decades, so it appears that teachers have benefited by the competition between their two competing federations. As organized teacher relationships have matured, however, local organizations of the NEA and the AFT have begun to merge in a few cities. In addition, the two statewide organizations have recently merged in New York. If the NEA and the AFT ever merge nationally, the combined membership would make it the largest union of professional employees in the world.

Collective bargaining has made a significant impact on the financial circumstances of teacher employment. Salaries and compensation levels have improved markedly. In Michigan, for example, teacher salaries have risen by nearly 50 percent in the past five years and this experience is by no means unusual. Only about half of this increase can be directly attributed to collective bargaining since the other half reflects increases matching inflation that probably would have occurred in any event. It is nevertheless clear that, in the short run at least, the wage and fringe benefits of public employees increase more rapidly by collective bargaining than in its absence.

Problems concerning the appropriate subject matter for collective bargaining in the public sector are well characterized in teacher negotiations. In private sector negotiations, the quality of the product is generally considered to be the concern and prerogative of management. In the public sector, particularly in education, the quality of the product is usually determined in great part by performance at the point of delivery. Professional employees such as teachers have a strong interest in the quality of service they provide. Hence they frequently challenge management on matters sometimes said to be questions of basic educational policies: curricular reform, textbook selection, and student discipline. Moreover, there are issues such as class size and the length of the school year that are matters of educational policy as well as conditions of employment. As a result, teachers press strongly for collective agreements that either cover these matters or provide procedures to work out these issues. Some collective bargaining agreements now permit teachers to participate in evaluating probationary colleagues, require school boards to employ ancillary and support professionals, and envisage joint determination of curriculum changes. However, teacher pressure to expand negotiations to focus on these issues is viewed with alarm by many school administrators who feel that teacher union positions on these matters of educational policy reflect little more than the members' self-interest.

Teacher transfer policies and student discipline have racial and social implications far transcending the education sphere and many of these matters are also of concern to parents and the community as well as to school administrators and teachers. Several states have tried to approach this problem legislatively. Maine law stipulates that "public employers of teachers shall be required to meet and consult but not negotiate with respect to educational policies" with representatives of organized teachers. Such statutes reflect increasing exploration of the concept that many public policies of legitimate concern to professional employees should nevertheless be determined not solely through collective bargaining but through some kind of joint determination by all affected groups. But in the public sector to a much greater degree than in the private sector, it is extremely hard to draw the line between policymaking that should be the responsibility of officials and working conditions that should be set in negotiations.

Some continuing problems

A basic argument for the extension of collective bargaining rights to public sector employees in the United States is that rights mandated by law in the private sector should in equity be given to the government's own employees. This is not to suggest that there are not important differences between private and public employment, however, and that these differences have not created some difficult problems as the private sector bargaining model increasingly pervades the public sector.

Probably the most fundamental of these problems lies in the different purposes of public and private undertakings. The public employer is an artificial creature of the electorate established to minister to the needs and desires of the public and to provide the mechanical and administrative structure to carry on these functions. In a democratic system of government it is elected officials who are normally charged with the control and determination of budget and tax rates, which is the primary way of setting goals and priorities. While extra-parliamentary influences are both inevitable and necessary elements of the democratic process, they should not be allowed to obscure the fact that elected legislative bodies are supposed to be deliberative bodies. If democratic governments are to distinguish between public passions and public interests, legislatures have to be at least partially insulated from group pressures. In a number of major American cities the crisis pressures that result from actual or threatened withdrawal of public employment services have at times usurped the legislature's deliberative process in this most fundamental government function of setting goals and priorities.

A second problem lies in the existence of the merit and civil service systems in the public sector in the United States. These systems, basically designed to ensure that the selection, retention, and promotion of public employees are based on qualifications and meritorious performace alone, are often considered to be the warp and woof of public employment. To employees, however, merit rating is sometimes considered a euphemism for favoritism. Public employee organizations therefore attempt to negotiate strict seniority, across-the-board wage adjustments, and the like. It is an unsettled question whether civil service and merit systems can survive the assault of traditional collective bargaining practices. But it is clear that protection of the public employees' right to continued employment, assuming meritorious service, is increasingly being enforced through negotiated grievance procedures culminating in binding neutral arbitration rather than through statutory devices such as the tenure system.

A third general problem is that of unions for supervisory staff. In private industry in the United States the lines of authority and supervision are usually clearly drawn, even in the areas of white-collar employment. In the public sector, however, the lines between supervisor and employee are far more indistinct. The appellation of supervisor tends to be pushed further down in the organizational hierarchy in public than in private bureaucracies. Where all are dedicated to serving the public, there is a greater community of interest among all employees. In the public service, supervisors and nonsupervisors are often compensated within an identical and fairly rigid salary structure. As a reflection of these facts many existing state collective bargaining laws have not drawn the traditional distinctions between supervisors and employees. Thus labor relations boards that implement the state laws have permitted supervisory unionism. In some cases they have required the recognition of supervisory units as components of the same union that organizes those who are supervised. Whether conflict of interest is inevitable between the supervisory goals of the organization and the fraternal goals of the union is as yet uncertain. It is clearly a danger, however.

A fourth serious problem in public employee bargaining arises because of the diffusion of decision-making authority that frequently exists in the public sector. Parliamentary systems of government permit a greater unity of legislative and executive authority than is common in United States government systems where a division of authority between the executive and legislative is more often characteristic. A head of a federal, state, or local government agency may have authority to negotiate on only a portion of the issues that are normally subjects of collective bargaining; other negotiable subjects may be retained within the control of the legislative body or an independent civil service board. Often a chief executive may not have final authority regarding the distribution of funds and can only submit recommendations to the appropriate legislature. May the legislative body repudiate his decisions? Does it have to provide the funds to pay for the salary structure he has negotiated? Finally, where voter approval of increased millage is necessary to pay for the negotiated increases, local taxpayers revolts are increasingly common. What is to be done in these situations? Questions of this kind are extremely difficult to answer within many, although not all, governments in the United States. But the internal logic of public employee bargaining is leading to considerable centralization of power and to increased executive power vis-a-vis legislatures and civil service boards.

Related to but distinguishable from the previous problem is one characterized as "end-run" or "double-deck" bargaining. Some public employee unions attempt by lobbying to secure from the state legislature those items they did not obtain or have traded away at the municipal bargaining table. In many states, civil service organizations have formed one of the strongest lobbies in the state legislature. These powers can hardly be taken away from such organizations. But from the municipal government's point of view, freedom to trade cost reductions in one area for contractually bargained new expenditures in another is an essential element of bargaining flexibility and bargaining equality. State legislatures that mandate wage and fringe bargaining at the municipal level and continue to legislate on municipal employee benefits place local units of government in a Procrustean bed. Public employee bargaining may be desirable and inevitable, but public employees hardly seem entitled to the benefits both of collective bargaining and of traditional protective state laws.

A final problem of collective bargaining in the public sector is that of public employee strikes. Most contemporary discussions of this subject in the United States concern the issue of whether public employees have or should be given the legal right to strike. The fact is, of course, that despite *de jure* absence of this right in almost all governmental jurisdictions, in practice they can and do strike, often with impunity. Moreover, although it is not commonly recognized, the public employee strike problem exists both in jurisdictions that permit collective bargaining and in those that have not yet done so.

The public employee strike problem is not overwhelming on a national basis. In the last decade such strikes have grown in frequency from approximately one per month to one per day in the whole nation, but strike activity in the public sector is still far below that in the private sector. Public employees involved in work stoppages in recent years represent about 1.5 percent of total employment, compared to nearly 4 percent in the private sector. In 1970, the most recent year for which data are available, strike idleness represented .08 percent of man-days worked by government employees; for the economy as a whole this figure was .28 percent. The average duration of public employee strikes is less than five days for what might be termed "essential" employees; for those in less crucial occupations the average duration is over twice as long. Among teachers, the absolute number of strikes has declined substantially in the past two years.

Mediation and nonbinding neutral recommendations by so-called fact finders are the most common governmental devices used to help resolve collective bargaining impasses. While they are effective in the large majority of disputes, they are obviously not a panacea. Where it is deemed that no strike can be permitted, as is almost invariably the decision with police and firemen, compulsory binding arbitration is the most frequently used alternative. Eight states are now experimenting with variants of this device. The newest, although largely untested, idea in compulsory arbitration is "final offer selection," in which the arbitrator is given no power to compromise issues in dispute, but must select one or the other of the parties' final offers.

Conclusion

The coming of collective bargaining to the public sector is the most significant development in the industrial relations field in the United States in the last 30 years. Its growth has been both rapid and extensive and appears to be continuing. Even now, however, bargaining does not occur in more than half of all governmental jurisdictions in the United States. In many areas where bargaining has begun it is less than ten years old. Hence one must be cautious in making generalizations about the future of public employee labor relations. A few may be put forward tentatively, however.

The coming of unionism to the public sector has provided enough new recruits to the labor movement to reverse the decline in trade union membership that took place during the late 1950s and early 1960s. Moreover, it is at least possible that as government employees join unions, or as their traditional professional associations begin to behave more like unions, this will change the general blue-collar image of the labor movement in the United States. Private sector trade unionism has never exceeded 30 percent of the nonagricultural workforce and has never had any strong appeal to white-collar workers. Organizing successes among white-collar and professional employees in the public sector may make unionism acceptable and normal to private sector white-collar workers who in the near future, if they do not already, will represent a majority of employment in private industry. In summary, public employee unionism has halted the decline in trade union membership in the United States and may in fact contribute to substantial new growth in the private sector in the next decade or two.

Public employee unionism appears to have contributed to the centralization of governmental decision-making power in the United States, although it is by no means the sole cause of such developments. At the municipal level it is clear that the exigencies of collective bargaining have forced decision-making power towards the chief executive at the expense of municipal legislatures and civil service boards. In the educational field, pressures exerted by organized teachers along with a number of constitutional decisions are forcing a shift away from the local property tax towards the state-imposed income tax as the primary means of financing public education. Almost inevitably this will mean that many financial decisions will be removed from local school boards and centralized in intermediate or statewide decision-making bodies. At the federal level the movement toward nation-wide bargaining units of federal civil servants may slow or halt efforts for federal decentralization that were initiated in the 1960s. In short, public employee unionism appears in many areas to be leading to more centralized decision making in the United States as it has in many other industrialized democracies.

The economic results of public employee bargaining are as yet unclear and controversial. Some authorities believe that public employees have driven their salary and benefit levels far higher than would have been the case in the absence of collective bargaining, and higher than can be justified on the basis of economic equity. Others challenge this assumption. They state that recent increases in public employee compensation are largely reflective of inflationary pressures in American society and the need for public employees to "catch up" with others whose wages and salaries should be comparable. Quantitative data that would support either argument are still scanty. Public employees in some occupations clearly have fared more favorably in recent years than has the average employee in the private sector. The differences are not large, however, and during 1971 and 1972, increases in both sectors were held down by government wages policies.

As yet, at least, the impact of public employee unionism on governmental decision making has not been as great as the numerical increase in public union membership and bargaining unit growth might suggest. In the federal sector it is estimated that employees have the right to bargain on perhaps only 25 percent of the subjects that are negotiable in the private sector. Although the scope of bargaining is increasing at the federal level, and is already more extensive at the local and educational levels, it cannot be said with any certainty that the large majority of governmental and public policy decisions are fundamentally different from what they would have been in the absence of collective bargaining.

Finally, and most speculatively, it is possible that public employee unionism will bring changes to the whole of the labor relations environment in the United States. As previously noted, white-collar and professional organization in the public sector may bring a greater acceptability of white-collar unionization in the private sector. If devices such as compulsory arbitration become common and effective for resolving collective bargaining impasses in the public sector, their use may increasingly be urged in the private sector. In general, and with many obvious exceptions, public sector labor relations practices and laws in the United States have thus far been strongly modeled on private sector structures that evolved earlier. Over time, experience in the public sector may prove that certain procedures and practices, now uncommon or unknown in the private sector, are useful or effective. It is not at all unlikely that such practices might then become acceptable in the private sector. In sum, the future may well be one of simultaneous change in both sectors, each tending generally to become more like the other.

3

Wage Determination in the National Public Service in Japan: Changes and Prospects

*Kazutoshi Koshiro**

O F the 106 million total population, 52 million people were in the Japanese labour force in 1972. Because of the large number of self-employed and family workers, wage and salaried employees in 1972 accounted for only 34,520,000, or just two-thirds, of the labour force.

Although the first Japanese labour union was organized in 1897, and the practice of collective bargaining was started in the early 1910s, the modern system of industrial relations was not established until after World War II when workers were given the right to strike with protection from criminal and civil prosecution.

The contemporary system of industrial relations in Japan can be classified into five categories if we look at the method of determining wages and working conditions. First, free collective bargaining with the right to strike covers 8,725,000 trade union members in the private sector, including public utilities workers employed by electric power and gas industries, private hospitals,

*Professor of Economics, Yokohama National University.

43

and private railways. Although their services are essential, these workers are entitled to the right to strike, which is limited only by the emergency procedures stipulated in the Labour Relations Adjustment Law of 1946. The right to strike of workers in coal mining, electricity, and maritime industries is also subject to some limits for safety purposes.

The second category includes public employees in the nationalized industries who are covered by a compulsory arbitration system. About 1.2 million workers are employed in the three public corporations (National Railways, Telephone and Telegram, and Tobacco Monopoly) and five national enterprises (Postal Service, National Forestry, Alcohol Monopoly, Mint, and Government Printing Office). Another 300,000 workers are employed in local public enterprises such as transport, water supply, hospitals, sewage, harbors, etc. These two groups do not have the right to strike but they can determine their wages and working conditions through collective bargaining. In case of impasses, their labour disputes are to be settled through mediation, fact-finding, or arbitration by the Public Corporation and National Enterprise Labour Relations Commission *(Korōi)*, or local labour relations commissions (in the case of local enterprises). Since no strike actions are permitted for these public workers, dispute settlement procedures are compulsory and the arbitration award is both final and binding for the parties concerned. However, the government, which is not the employer of these public workers, cannot spend money beyond the budgets authorized by the Diet (or local assemblies in the case of local enterprises). In Japan, the budgets of public corporations and national enterprises are authorized by the Diet and, if additional financing is necessary for the implementation of collective bargaining agreements or arbitration awards in these firms, the government must ask for authorization from the Diet beforehand. Although it is understood that such financial control by the Diet is indispensable for democratic determination of the budget, it has led to severe confrontations between the government and public employee unions because of reduced implementation of the arbitration awards of the labour commission until 1957. The details and the results of such disputes, as well as the reasons for the shift in 1957, will be described below.

The third category includes national and local civil servants whose pay and working conditions are determined by law. About 800,000 national civil service employees (including 280,-000 members of the defense forces) and 2,300,000 local civil service employees (including 800,000 teachers and 180,000 policemen) are covered by this system. The National Personnel Authority is responsible for protecting and maintaining a reasonable standard of pay comparable to the average pay levels in private industries for the 450,000 "ordinary grades" national civil service employees. Since 1948, sophisticated techniques and procedures have been developed for this purpose. Salaries of the "special grades" national civil service employees, which includes members of the defense forces, judges, and ministers, reflect the changes of pay schedules for the "ordinary grades" national civil service employees subject to the resolutions by the Diet. Similarly, the salaries of local civil servants employed in the prefectural governments and municipalities are to be revised according to the recommendations of the local civil service commission (or equity commission) in each locality. However, the recommendations of these local commissions tend to automatically follow the average rate of increase for the national civil service recommended by the National Personnel Authority.

Several problems do exist, of course, for the pay determination of local civil servants for whom equity with the national civil service at the level of comparable jobs is vitally important. The most powerful employee organizations in the local civil service are the 930,000-strong *Jichiro* (All Japan Prefectural and Municipal Workers' Union) and the 570,000-strong *Nikkyoso* (Japan Teachers' Union), the two largest unions in Japan. On the other hand, policemen and firemen are not allowed to organize into unions. Since the problems of pay determination for the local civil service are too complicated to deal with in this limited space, the author should point out one feature that seems unique to Japan: the considerable extent of pay differentials among prefectures or municipalities based on the different financial conditions of each local government.

The fourth system involves wage determination by wage boards. Since 1958, each prefecture has established several boards to determine minimum wages at the industry level. There is also a nation-wide wage board for coal miners. Wage boards have come to play an increasing role in fixing minimum wages since the 1968 reform of the minimum wage law. This system covers about 16 million workers in the private industries. However, some organized workers are dually covered by the wage boards and free collective bargaining. It would, perhaps, be safe to say that about 7 million workers in the unorganized small firms are covered solely by the wage boards.

The last category encompasses the 14 million workers who are not covered by any of the above practices and who must rely on individual labour contracts with their respective employers. Once the collective bargaining system and the legal system of wage determination have been introduced for other employees, the determination of wages and salaries for remaining employees will, of course, be influenced by these organized methods. However, the largest single group of employees are still unprotected by either of the organized methods of pay determination.

Before entering into the subject of this paper, some major features of industrial relations common to both the private and public sectors should be reviewed.

(1) Collective bargaining is concentrated at the enterprise level. National or other geographically-based organizations play only a minor role. Theoretically, collective bargaining in the public sector is limited within each agency (for example, the National Railways or the Department of Postal Service).

(2) In 1955, several small, segmented industrial unions initiated a cooperative effort to compensate for their organizational weakness and to enhance their spring wage demands. Unions of the public corporations and the national enterprises joined in the "spring wage offensive" in 1957. Moreover, these public employee unions have, at times, used "work-to-rule" practices or overt illegal walk-outs to press for favourable wage increases for other public sector as well as private sector workers.

(3) Not withstanding the above, most wage disputes in the private sector are settled peacefully. Strikes for wages usually con-

tinue for only a few hours or a few days at the most, although several protracted strikes have occurred over issues concerning the dismissal of large numbers of nonessential workers. Private industry employers are more threatened by the diffusion of political unionism from public employees into private enterprise strongholds.

(4) There is generally no distinction within the bargaining unit between blue-collar and white-collar workers in different occupations or crafts. Indeed, the demarcation between various crafts or occupations is quite alien to Japanese trade unionism. In the public sector, although there are different salary schedules according to classifications, the bargaining units or union demarcations do not correspond to these classifications. Manual workers, lower clerical employees, and candidates for higher civil service positions belong to the same union if they are employed in the same department or agency.

Declining influence of public employee unionism

Labour relations in the public sector served as a pattern for the private sector throughout the 1950s. However, in the 1960s and 1970s, employment and union membership increased more rapidly in the private sector than in the public sector. Public employment represented about 20 percent of the total employment in the early 1950s but steadily declined so that it accounted for only 13 percent by 1971. Only a fourth of all union members belonged to the public sector in 1971, whereas in the 1950s more than a third of the public employees had been members of unions (Table 1). In addition to these changes, economic growth and a labour shortage stimulated the development of autonomous collective bargaining in the private sector and made the public sector follow wage increases set in private industries. The principle of comparability of pay between the two sectors, introduced in 1948, has been reformed considerably in many branches of public employment.

Public employee unions have played a leading role in the post-war labour movement in Japan. They still hold a majority in the most powerful national labour centre, *Sohyo* (General

Council of Japanese Trade Unions of Japan) . However, *Sohyo's* influence has been declining since the late 1960s.

There are now 11.8 million organized employees in Japan, 34.9 percent of the total number of employees (34 million) . Many of the enterprise unions are affiliated with one of the four national trade union centres: *Sohyo* with 4.2 million members or 36 percent of the total unionized labour force: *Domei* (Japanese Confederation of Labour) with 2.2 million or 18 percent; *Churitsuroren* (Federation of Independent Unions) with 1.3 million or 11 percent; and *Shinsanbetsu* (National Federation of Industrial Organizations) with only 76,000 or 0.6 percent. The last two national labour centres do not have a significant number of members in the public sector. The remaining 4.1 million, or 35 percent, of the unionists do not belong to any of the four national centres; they are also employed primarily in the private sector.

In its heyday in 1960, *Sohyo* accounted for 49 percent of organized labour with a membership of 3,750,000. Although *Sohyo* has been able to increase its numbers continuously, it has suffered numerous setbacks in relative terms, especially since 1967, when it began to lose members in the private sector. *Domei* has now surpassed *Sohyo* in terms of membership within the private sector.

Comparing *Sohyo* and *Domei* in terms of public sector-private sector membership distribution, *Sohyo's* total membership of 4.2 million consists of 2.6 million public service workers (62 percent) and 1.6 million private sector workers (38 percent) . On the other hand, 92 percent of *Domei's* total membership of 2.2 million comes from the private sector. *Sohyo's* problems lie in the fact that its organizational structure is oriented toward public service workers. The national unions from the private sector form a minority group within *Sohyo* and now stand firmly against *Sohyo's* present leaders, demanding that they carry out drastic changes in the structure as well as the policies of the organization. It is anticipated that about 6 million unionists in the private sector, including those from *Sohyo*, will be reunified into a new federation in the near future, which will exclude the public employee unions within *Sohyo*.[1]

Table 1

Changes in the composition of union membership by employment (%)

Status	1953	1959	1965	1971
ORGANIZED WORKERS	5,927 (100.0)	7,211 (100.0)	10,147 (100.0)	11,798 (100.0)
Private sector	3,822 (64.5)	4,652 (64.5)	7,209 (71.1)	8,713 (73.9)
Public sector	2,105 (35.5)	2,559 (35.5)	2,938 (28.9)	3,085 (26.1)
National civil service	221 (3.7)	273 (3.8)	256 (2.5)	284 (2.4)
Local civil service	951 (16.1)	1,236 (17.1)	1,500 (14.8)	1,588 (13.5)
Public corporations, etc	861 (14.5)	933 (12.9)	1,005 (9.9)	1,020 (8.6)
Local public enterprises	73 (1.2)	118 (1.6)	178 (1.7)	192 (1.6)
TOTAL NUMBER OF EMPLOYEES	16,600 (100.0)	22,500 (100.0)	28,760 (100.0)	34,060 (100.0)
Private sector	13,661 (82.3)	19,220 (85.4)	24,616 (85.6)	29,525 (86.7)
Public sector	2,939 (17.7)*	3,280 (14.6)	4,144 (14.4)	4,535 (13.3)

*In 1950, the number of public employees was 2,913,000 or 20.7 percent of the total number of all employees (14,063,000).

Source: The Ministry of Labor, *Basic Survey of Trade Unions,* and Prime Minister's Office, *Labor Force Survey.* The number of public employees is compiled from various official sources. (K. Koshiro, *Wage Determination in Japan's Public Sector,* Tokyo: Nippon Hyoron Sha, 1973, p. 17 and Appendix 3.)

Intensified activities for the restoration of the right to strike by the public employee unions

The cleavage between private and public sector unionism has been aggravated since 1965 when the public employee unions in *Sohyo* began intensified activities for the restoration of the right to strike. The industrial public employees were deprived of the right to strike in July 1948, by order of General MacArthur, Supreme Commander of the Allied Powers. (It should be mentioned that after a short period of freedom nonindustrial civil servants had already been deprived of their right to strike by the Labour Relations Adjustment Law in September 1946.

Since 1957, industrial public employee unions such as the National Railway Workers, Locomotive Engineers of the National Railway, and Postal Workers have pressed for the restoration of the right to strike. Their concern has become more intense since 1965, when the government ratified the ILO Convention No. 87 concerning freedom of association and protection of the right to organize. Since then, they have been prone to conducting work-to-rule practices, especially during the spring offensive for wage hikes (Table 2). Moreover, they have often engaged in various types of industrial actions to protest disciplinary sanctions by the authorities. This vicious circle culminated in mass discharges in the National Railway and Postal Service in September 1972.[2]

In 1965, the ILO Fact Finding and Conciliation Commission on Freedom of Association as set forth by ILO Convention No. 87 (the Dreyer Commission) strongly recommended that distinctions should be made between public enterprises according to the essentiality of their services.[3] It also criticized the extreme demands of public employee unions that sought to gain the unrestricted right to strike.[4] The demand for "total restoration" of the right to strike for public employees and the "absolute prohibition" of the right to strike were both condemned by the Commission as "unduly rigid and unrealistic."[5]

The government established a tripartite council in October 1965 to consider ways to implement the Commission's recommendations. The council is now in its third term and a realistic

Table 2

The number of public employees engaged in dispute actions

Year	Number of Dispute Actions in the Public Service	Number of Public Employees Engaged in Dispute Actions (in thousands)
1965	223	90
1966	536	264
1967	10	6
1968	520	352
1969	1,133	607
1970	344	110
1971	1,694	538

Source: Ministry of Labour, *Statistics of Labour Disputes.*

compromise has still not been reached. However, the new LDP administration is committed to resolving these disputes over labour relations in the public sector.[6]

Since 1966, several courts have decided in favour of union members who were previously criminally prosecuted and/or discharged by authorities.[7] These courts adopted a new criterion for distinguishing illegal strike actions from those that "do not likely endanger the public life to a serious extent." The essentiality of the services as such, as well as the forms and methods of the strikes have been taken into account in judging the illegality of specific cases.

Several local courts have accepted this criterion and some have declared further that, in such cases, public employees should be exempted from administrative prosecutions and should not be automatically discharged or disciplined. The Supreme Court, in a decision on April 25, 1973, rejected these new standards and supported the principle that public employees should not be allowed to strike or to instigate strike actions because they are the servants of the whole society. The Court insisted that present devices which compensate for denying public employees the right to strike are satisfactory and reasonable.

Certainly, the compulsory arbitration system for employees of public corporations and national enterprises has improved since

1957 and the comparability of pay for the civil service has been maintained rather effectively through recommendations by the National Personnel Authority since 1960. But the justification by the Court for the overall prohibition of the right to strike for public employees cannot necessarily be supported.

On April 27, 1973, only two days after the new Supreme Court decision, the government compromised and agreed to sign a memorandum with representatives of public employee unions. Although the memorandum was deliberately written in very vague terms, it could imply that the government would admit the right to strike for some public corporations (such as the tobacco monopoly) and national enterprises (such as the national forestry and alcohol monopolies). It is also suggested in some quarters that status distinctions will have to be made within the civil service for collective bargaining to be acceptable.[8]

However, public employee unions also have not been realistic in preparing to cope with anticipated reforms in the legal framework. What is the most appropriate bargaining unit? How should pay differentials be maintained or revised according to agencies or occupations? How can really serious strikes be controlled? Are the unions ready to accept the strike prohibition for designated employees? What would be the future function of the National Personnel Authority and the Public Corporation Labour Relations Commission? Are they to be eliminated or reformed? These are only a few of the major questions which remain unanswered even after the recommendation of the Advisory Council on the Public Personnel System. It does not appear that the unions have seriously considered many of them.

Wage determination for the employees of public corporations and national enterprises

In June 1971, there were about 1.2 million workers employed in the three public corporations and five national enterprises; 1,020,000 were organized in unions. They can determine wages and other working conditions through collective bargaining without the right to strike. There are two dimensions to wage negotiation: the rate of wage increase and the distribution of the increased pay among union members. The former has, in practice, been determined through compulsory arbitration by the Public Corporation and National Enterprise Labour Relations Commission. The latter has been negotiated to a considerable extent in each firm, sometimes accompanied by short-term strikes.

In the first stage (1949–1956), the government did not always fully accept arbitration awards because of financial limitations which, in turn, provoked irreconcilable distrust on the part of the unions. In the second stage (1957–1965), the Minister of Labour persuaded the government to modify its labour policy in the public corporations; the government then began to accept arbitration awards and to ask the legislature for the necessary appropriations. At the same time, however, the government encouraged management to discipline employees involved in illegal industrial actions. Management refused to negotiate with dismissed union officials based on a provision of the law. The disputes eventually culminated with the ratification of ILO Convention No. 87 in 1965. In the third stage (1965 to the present), the vicious circle of "illegal disputes" and mass disciplinary actions still continues.

However, aside from the confrontation concerning the right to strike, there have been remarkable improvements in wage settlements since 1961. (1) The arbitration awards for wage increases in 1961 were generous enough to become a pattern for the private sector. (2) Prime Minister Ikeda met with *Sohyo* Chairman Ohta in 1964 and reaffirmed the pay principle that employees of public corporations and national enterprises were entitled to wages comparable to those of the private sector. The agreement meant that pay differentials between industrial public employees and private industrial workers should be eliminated. The comparability principle has been respected by the government ever since. (3) Although final settlements have been formally attained through compulsory arbitration, substantial agreements have been worked out since 1967 through tripartite fact-finding panels. The chairman of the panel usually publicizes an agreed rate of pay increase, which is awarded afterwards by the arbitration board. This is a device to develop voluntary negotiations by the parties concerned within the framework of public corporations having little financial autonomy.

Further improvements suggested by several experts are as follows: (1) A greater degree of financial autonomy·should be delegated to the authorities of public corporations, especially to the National Railway. At the same time, the enormous amount of its cumulative deficits should be the burden of the government. The local lines, which operate in the red due to various political considerations, should be reorganized into an agency separate from the National Railway. (2) A formal negotiating body, consisting of representatives of government (Secretary General of the Cabinet, Ministers of Finance and Labour, etc.) and of the managements of public corporations and national enterprises, should be established, although the ultimate authority of the legislature concerning financial appropriations should be retained. (3) The right of employees to strike should be granted at least to the industrial employees of public firms. (4) More responsible activities on the part of unions are indispensable. They should refrain from industrial actions during mediation or fact finding.

In order to realize these improvements, the Public Corporation and National Enterprise Labour Relations Law, especially section 17 which stipulates the strike ban, will have to be revised. Union rivalries due to ideological competition must also be taken into account in order to normalize labour relations in this field.

Issues in the national civil service

The method of pay determination for the national civil service is a mixture of occidental and oriental systems. It is oriental because a highly unilateral formula is applied in the process beginning with a wage survey of private sector employees and including fixing of pay rates for each job. At the same time, it is occidental because it was suggested and implanted by the Occupation Forces after World War II. American influence, among others, is dominant in the structure and function of the National Personnel Authority. However, since the Occupation, it has been revised, modified, and adapted to Japanese conditions. Its workings are democratic and autocratic at the same time.

There were 459,399 national civil servants in March 1972; 10 percent were in executive, administrative, and supervisory positions and do not have the right to organize. Of the eligible employees, about 50 percent are organized. They are classified into ten pay schedules that represent major occupational groups: general administrative occupations, general operative occupations, educational occupations, medical doctors, nurses, seamen, tax-collectors, national police, etc. However, these occupational groups as such are not reflected in the union structure. The unions are organized on an agency-by-agency basis and are therefore multioccupational, corresponding to the employer rather than to the job.

National civil servants have neither the right to collective bargaining nor the right to strike. Even the elevator operators and janitors are denied these rights. Therefore, as compensation for the strike ban, the Authority is required to recommend necessary pay adjustments to the government and legislature. If the cost of living and/or the public-private pay differentials go up more than 5 percent, the Authority must recommend appropriate pay hikes. However, the recommendation is not binding on the government and, in fact, the recommended pay increases were not implemented to the full extent until 1970. (If we set aside the retroactive payment, the recommended pay hikes have been fully retroactive since 1960.)

Two principles are applied in pay determination by the Authority: (a) comparability with private employment and (b) equity within the service. The procedures to implement these principles, used since 1960 by the Authority, are as follows: First, in April the Authority surveys pay rates for each job in private firms that have more than 100 employees,[9] (in the case of multiestablishment firms, each establishment must have more than 50 employees). For example, 7,250 establishments employing 3,600,000 employees were selected as a sample to represent 60 percent of the total private employees in 1972. Second, the pay differentials between the two sectors are calculated by the "Laspeyres Formula," taking into account job content, educational level, age, sex, and regional composition of the labour force. It was 10.68 percent higher in the private sector in 1972. Third, the resulting aggregate pay differentials indicate the average percentage rate of increased payroll or wage adjustment fund that is necessary to maintain comparable pay levels with the private sector as a whole. Therefore, the wage adjustment fund should be distributed among the different pay schedules, grades and steps within each grade according to the second principle. The precise methods of achieving equitable pay levels within the service are not published officially; they seem to be rather mysterious. Fourth, the Authority recommends the revised pay schedules to the government and legislature.

Compared with English, Canadian, or American (since 1970) systems of pay research, at least one factor is unique in Japan: alienation of the employee organizations from the formal process of pay research by the Authority. The unions within the national civil service, as well as local civil service (especially teachers whose standards of pay are directly controlled by the central government), can confer and meet often with the Authority. But they cannot participate formally in the process of pay research.

Several technical problems have been raised for further improvements: The establishments to be surveyed in the private sector by the Authority should be those employing more than 1,000 workers rather than 50; the standard of living is underestimated by the Authority; coercive integration of several occupations under a single system sacrifices the interests of doctors, scientists, and professors, etc.

The overall prohibition of strikes in the national civil service from deputy secretary down to office boy has been denounced by the unions. Nevertheless, there is little prospect for the restoration of the right to strike for even a part of the service (the general operative grade contains chauffeurs, technicians, and other manual workers).[10] The political climate has been and will continue to be conservative, at least in the near future. Unions have indulged in political activities rather than in economic activities for their members. Neglect of professional interests, along with the professionals' feeling of exclusion from unions

that emphasize class consciousness, prevent the unions from finding more appropriate forms of representation. Without such
representation, wage determination by collective bargaining,
even if possible, will not work effectively. This seems to explain
why half of those eligible in the national civil service stay out of
the unions.

Direction of developments: summary

(1) Unlike most western countries, employment in Japan's public sector is not increasing relative to the total labour force. The
percentage of employees in the public sector has declined from
about 20 percent after World War II to about 13 percent in recent years. Moreover, it is extremely unlikely that any more industries will be nationalized in the near future.

(2) In Japan, the concept of the civil servant is much
broader than it is in most other countries. Before the war, civil
servants were divided into three groups based on the German
system: *Kanri (Beamte), Koin (Angestellte)* and *Yonin (Arbeiter)*. However, in the postwar period, Japan switched to the
more inclusive American system. Thus, even elevator operators
and janitors are included in the Japanese civil service and are
thereby deprived of the right to bargain collectively or to strike.

The concept of the public employee is also very broad and includes many types of industrial employees in such nationalized
industries as postal service, national railways, telecommunications, cigarette making, etc. Although some of these employees are not closely bound up with the daily livelihood of the
people, they are prohibited from going on strike.

On the other hand, essential services provided by medical doctors, nurses, and other workers in the private hospitals are distinguished from those in the public hospitals. Legally, employees
in private hospitals are free to strike in spite of the fact that
most of their income comes from the government's health insurance system. Indeed, in order to hike the fees for their medical
services, doctors in private hospitals have quit the health insurance system en masse.

(3) The public agencies and corporations in Japan have very

little independence to negotiate directly with labour. This is especially true with regard to matters of wage rates. Even in the case of public corporations, financial control by both the Diet and the central government is very tight. Friction between labour and management in the public sector has resulted. Many have suggested that management in public corporations should be given enough latitude to freely reallocate financial resources within the limit of an agreed upon budget.

(4) Many public employees are organized into their own unions at each ministry or agency. Most of these public sector unions are affiliated with *Sohyo,* which also has affiliates in the private sector. The local government employees' union and the teacher's union are the largest "industrial unions" in Japan, together having over 1.5 million members. Their influence on the labour movement as a whole has been considerable. Coupled with other powerful public sector unions, especially those in the railways and postal service, the public sector undoubtedly has a strong impact on labour unions in the private sector.

On the other hand, employers in the public sector do not have formal ties with private employers' associations, nor do they have any official association of their own. However, employers of the three public corporations and the five national enterprises maintain close contact to discuss their common problems with the labor unions.

(5) As we have seen, Japanese public employees, especially those in the nationalized industries, have been demanding that their right to strike, which was rescinded in 1948 by the GHQ, be restored.

This dispute has continued since 1957. The unions first appealed to the ILO in 1958, which finally sent a fact-finding and conciliation commission (the Dreyer Commission) to Japan in January 1965. The unions complained that the government was limiting the freedom of public employees to associate. Following the Dreyer Commission's visit, the Japanese government ratified ILO Convention No. 87 in May 1965. However, efforts to differentiate between public employees whose service has a direct bearing on the daily livelihood of the people and those whose service does not, have not been successful. This is in spite of the fact that discussions had been carried on for eight years (until September 1973) by a tripartite deliberation council that was set up following ratification of the ILO Convention No. 87.

(6) There is some possibility that unions for national and local civil service workers will be allowed to participate formally in the pay surveys conducted by the National Personnel Authority and by local personnel commissions depending upon the recommendations of that deliberative council. But it is unlikely that the right to collective bargaining will be extended to the national and local civil service in the near future. In the case of public corporations, more autonomy in collective bargaining may be granted to management and the right to strike may be restored, in some limited form, to some of the nationalized industries. But even with the right to strike partially restored, there is little chance that workers will be allowed to participate in the management of the nationalized industries. At present, there are no auditors or members of the board of directors from labour in either the public or the private sector.

(7) It is widely understood by most government officials that an incomes policy will not realistically serve to control inflation unless something is done beforehand to restrain the skyrocketing land prices. However, it is still possible to restrain public employees' pay hikes in order to dampen the demand for higher wages in the private sector. If the annual rate of real economic growth drops drastically to a level of "zero growth," or if the international balance of payments deteriorates beyond a certain point, an incomes policy may be considered by the government.

1. As a result of the strong setback suffered by the Democratic Socialist Party (supported by *Domei*) in the general election in December 1972, the movement to reunify the labour front faced a number of obstacles. In contrast, the moderate advance of the Japan Socialist Party and strong showing of the Japan Communist Party strengthened *Sohyo's* forces and made negotiations for reunification even more complex. (K. Koshiro, "The Political Influence of Labor Unions in the General Elections," *Japan Labor Bulletin*, February 1973, p. 8.)

2. Forty-three union officials who were employees of the Japanese National Railways and three officials who were employees of the Department of Postal Service were dismissed. In addition, 38,772 railway employees and 1,884 postal workers were disciplined. The Postal Workers Union and other public

employee unions brought these matters to the attention of the ILO on October 6, 1972. The ILO Committee on Freedom of Association examined these appeals and submitted its final report to the ILO Governing Body on November 9, 1973. The Governing Body accepted the report on November 16. The report included several recommendations to both the unions and the Japanese government. It criticized the government's attitude on mass disciplinary actions against the participants in the illegal strikes." However, it also criticized the politically motivated strikes by the public employee unions.

It concluded with a statement of its hope that the Japanese government would take appropriate action in the near future to conform with the recent recommendations of the Advisory Council on the Public Personnel System (see footnote 6 below) and the principles stipulated in the ILO Conventions Nos. 87 and 98.

It should be added that another 156,774 public employees were disciplined by the authorities during the one year following the unions' appeal to the ILO in October 1972, including 58 union officials who were dismissed and 1,409 others who were suspended. Other union members received reduced salaries or reprimands.

3. Report of the Commission (Geneva: ILO, 1965), Paragraph 2140, p. 715.

4. *Ibid.,* Paragraph 2134, p. 713.

5. *Ibid.,* Paragraph 2135, p. 713.

6. The Advisory Council on the Public Personnel System published its final report and recommendations on September 3, 1973. The main points are as follows: With respect to the right to organize, further studies should be made regarding the right to organize for public firemen. Concerning the registration of unions, the government should not refuse to negotiate with unregistered organizations without reasonable grounds. With regard to collective bargaining, the authorities of the three public corporations and five national enterprises should be given more authority. The National Personnel Authority should consider employees' opinions in its recommendations on wages for the national civil service.

The right to strike was the most debated issue and the Council failed to achieve a consensus among its members. Three views were summarized in the report. With regard to nonindustrial clerical workers, one opinion argued that they should not be granted the right to strike under the present system. Another viewpoint suggested that the right to strike should be given to all such workers except those in charge of administrative work or jobs essential to the everyday livelihood of the people. The third way of thinking called for the right to strike for all. With regard to industrial field workers, one opinion claimed that none of them should be given the right to strike. Another viewpoint argued that the right to strike should be given to those whose work does not directly affect the everyday livelihood of the public. The third way of thinking argued that everybody should be allowed to strike under certain conditions and after having gone through certain procedures.

It is generally expected that it will take another few years to solve the points still left unclear in the recommendations.

7. The Supreme Court decision concerning the Central Post Office case, October 26, 1966; another decision concerning the Tokyo Teachers' Union

case, April 2, 1969; a third decision concerning the Sendai High Court case, April 2, 1969; and four other decisions by local courts in 1971 are relevant to public employees in the same area.

8. However, the recommendations of the Advisory Council on the Public Personnel System did not include acceptance of the idea of collective bargaining in the civil service. See footnote 6 above.

9. Until 1968, pay comparisons were made with private establishments (instead of firms) having more than 50 employees. In Japanese labour statistics, "establishment" is limited to the plant or factory, while "firm" implies the company as a whole.

10. The case of seamen exemplifies the problem. The majority of seamen are employed in private maritime companies and have the right to bargain collectively and to strike. Some, who are employed in the National Railway's ferry-boats, have only the right to collective bargaining. About 2,000 seamen are employed in the national civil service, and do not have either of these rights.

4

Labour Relations
in the Public Sector
in the United Kingdom

*David Winchester**

I N recent years, there has been a growing concern with the alleged deficiencies of the British system of industrial relations
and their contribution to the almost perennial economic difficulties of the country. This has given rise to increasing criticism of
long-established institutions and labour practices and to a number of radical innovations in the industrial policies of successive
governments. Attention has been primarily focussed on the problems of private manufacturing industries: the number of uncon-
stitutional strikes, restrictive labour practices, chaotic payment
systems and wage structures, and the urgent need for procedural
reform in collective bargaining. It was widely assumed that the
public sector was immune from such serious institutional difficulties, but the sharp rise in the incidence of industrial unrest that
has occurred in the last three years suggests a modification of
this view.[1]

It will be argued that while many of the employment problems in the public sector arise from circumstances common to

*Lecturer in Industrial Relations, The London School of Economics and
Political Science.

both private and public employment, attempts to resolve them are shaped by distinct political and organisational factors. Differences between public and private employment are not, however, reflected in the British system of labour law in any clear way. Legislation affecting particular groups of public employees has existed for more than a century, but as might be expected in an industrial relations system based so firmly on voluntarist principles, this has been much less important than rules and conventions developed by the parties themselves. In law, there is no clear separation between public and private employees or between public and private law.

Most of the literature on public sector labour relations in Britain is confined to particular parts of the sector. It tends to be largely descriptive, setting out in great detail the institutional development and formal procedures in the employment area under consideration, and rarely exploring the workplace behaviour of employees and management. The absence of many attempts to analyse the problems of the public sector as a whole is understandable as it comprises a highly diversified group of services and undertakings, each part reflecting its distinct historical evolution and traditions. Generalisations are more meaningful if three major categories of public employment are distinguished.

(1) Central or national government, known as the *Civil Service.* Employees are paid directly by money raised from taxation and may be manual or industrial workers (found in various maintenance, construction, or manufacturing jobs in government establishments) or nonindustrial civil servants (engaged in executive and administrative duties for government ministries).

(2) *Local authorities* of local government services. Employees are paid partly by local taxes or rates, although central government now provides more than half of local authority finance. They are engaged in a wide range of activities delegated by central government, including education, police, and fire protection; local transport; refuse collection; road and house building; recreational facilities, and many administrative duties.

(3) *Nationalised industries* or public corporations. Most of Britain's public corporations achieved this status in the period 1945–51 when the Labour Government nationalised many of the

fuel, power, and transport industries (electricity, gas, coal, railways, road haulage, and airlines) while the steel industry and the post office became public corporations in 1967–69.

These three major groupings provide some basis for generalisations about labour relations in the public sector, but they should not conceal the differences within each of the categories and some of the similarities between them. For example, an engineering craftsman may face similar employment conditions in national and local government and the nationalised industries, while within the group of nationalised industries there are enormous variations between the labour-intensive postal services and the technologically advanced electricity supply industry. However, on the crucial issue of the nature and extent of government interference in public sector employment relations, we shall see that the particular statutory obligations, finance, and organisation of these three groups result in distinct problems and differing consequences.

The most important period of growth for the public sector in Britain was during the 1945–51 post-war Labour Government. At this time, there was a rapid extension of the social services and the major fuel, power, and transport industries were brought under public ownership. Over the last 20 years, public sector employment has increased only slightly in aggregate terms, for much of this period comprising a declining percentage of an expanding work force. This overall relative stability conceals significant changes in employment within particular parts of the sector and in the occupational structure. For instance, there have been massive reductions in the coalmining and railway industries and continuous expansion of employment in the educational and health services. Generally speaking, the public services have expanded to form a larger part of the public sector relative to industries and public utilities (gas, electricity, and water supply) and the proportion of nonmanual employees is increasing throughout the sector. These trends may be expected to continue unless the Labour Party is re-elected to government office and carries out its pledge to extend public ownership considerably.

Table 1

Civilian employment in the public sector (in thousands)

	1960	*1965*	*1970*
Central Government	1,642	1,373	1,535
Local Authorities	1,737	2,040	2,467
Public Corporations	1,861	2,023	1,920
TOTAL	5,240	5,436	5,922

Management in the public sector

In the civil service, the most crucial managerial decisions, until recently, were made by the Treasury (Ministry of Finance). In 1969, a new independent ministry, the Civil Service Department, was established with a senior executive directly responsible to the Prime Minister. The Civil Service Department is responsible for developing policy on all labour relations issues: selection and recruitment, training, promotion, pay and conditions, administrative and managerial efficiency, and the coordination of pension arrangements throughout the public sector as a whole. The Treasury remains highly influential because of its role in budget allocation to various government departments, but the creation of the Civil Service Department may lead to a much greater specialisation of managerial functions compared with the previous position where personnel management was considered merely one of a number of administrative duties.[2]

The very high degree of centralisation and the almost overpowering pressure of uniformity in the civil service management contrasts somewhat with the situation found in the local government services. Here there is certainly central government influence over senior appointments and over particular services, for example, the police, fire, and education service, not least because central government provides some of the finance for the remuneration of local authority employees. However, considerable diversity in managerial structure, training, and policies exists among the 1,500 or more separate units that make up local government. Only the large, urban local authorities have developed any managerial professionalism and been exempted from widespread public criticism of their inefficiency in recent years. Local authorities have achieved some degree of co-ordination via membership in four national employers' associations and some uniformity in pay and employment conditions has been attained through the establishment of a central negotiating staff in 1948.

In April 1974, with the implementation of the Local Government Act of 1972, a new two-tier structure of local authorities became effective. In England and Wales, there are now 53 county authorities and 369 second-tier authorities outside London. The county authorities are responsible for public transport, highways, education and social services, and police and fire services; district authorities provide housing, water supply, sewerage, and refuse disposal services amongst other things. It is inevitable that these larger employing units will develop and rationalise managerial functions and expertise that are still primitive in most local authorities. A continuing potential source of strain will remain in the relationship between executive officers and the elected councillors in the new authorities, with the further political complication that in Britain's two-party political system it is now usual for a majority of major local councils to be governed by the political party in opposition to the central governing party.

The corporate structure of nationalised industries has been a subject of intense political controversy since the Labour Party first committed itself to a policy of the public ownership of key industries in 1918. In fact, the chosen vehicle of the 1945–51 Labour Government, the public corporation, reflected the enterprise structure of private industry. Public corporations were given a statutory duty to earn interest on capital and their management boards, although appointed by government ministers, were supposed to be free of political interference. In practice, all important policy areas are heavily influenced by government ministers, civil servants, or the Treasury, although the chairmen of some nationalised industries have been able to retain wider areas of autonomy than others. In recent years, governments have developed more explicit economic guidelines for public corporations: price, profit, and investment criteria, for example. These guidelines provide a framework of economic and financial constraints within which each corporation must operate, and by which its performance may be judged. If the government decides that these principles should be abandoned for political or social reasons (as in the maintenance of unprofitable railway services) then such exceptions may be financed by separate government grants or allowances. It also seems that governments are now stumbling towards some kind of coordination of nationalised industry policies—for example, a fuel and transport policy—rather than treating the public corporations as separate entities.[3]

Plant or workplace management in nationalised industries seems to have developed more sophisticated policies and techniques of personnel management than management in other parts of the public sector. Public ownership, per se, to the great disappointment of its strongest advocates, did not revolutionise management approaches to labour relations, but it helped to codify and generalise the better practices throughout some of the industries. In some respects, traditions that developed in industries before their nationalisation continue to flavour current labour and management practices. Most notably, in the steel industry, which was renationalised five years ago, many of the senior managerial positions are still held by members of the old "steel families" who fought valiantly to keep the industry in private ownership. At the same time, nationalised industries seem to attract individuals with a strong ideological preference for public rather than private industry into their higher managerial positions.

Labour organizations

Until the 1971 Industrial Relations Act, the impact of labour legislation on such issues as freedom of association, the recognition of trade unions, and their registration has been minimal or ambiguous in the United Kingdom. In practice, government policy has officially encouraged membership of trade unions and staff associations for half a century, so that labour organisation is far more extensive in the public than in the private sector. It also extends to much higher levels of the occupational hierarchy than in private manufacturing industries.

The nature and pattern of labour organisation is complex; examples of each structural type of trade union can be found in the various parts of the sector. In the industrial civil service, craft and general unions represent those trades and occupations that they organise elsewhere, while the nonmanual civil servants tend to be organised by occupational unions whose membership is confined to this sector. In local government, the two large general unions and a largely industrial union organise manual workers. The majority of nonmanual workers are represented by the National Association of Local Government Officers (NALGO) —probably the largest white-collar union in the world that has no members in the private sector. In the nationalised industries, there tends to be an embryonic industrial union in each part, but also general and craft unions and separate organisations covering nonmanual workers. There is, therefore, extensive multiunionism in all parts of the public sector and this will remain despite a reduction in the number of unions through amalgamation.

Multiunionism, per se, is not a very serious problem in the public sector. More significant are the differences between the organisation, ideology, and objectives of unions affiliated to the Trades Union Congress (TUC) and the Labour Party and those staff associations and professional associations that do not regard themselves as trade unions. After the 1926 General Strike, when associations of lower grade civil servants had implicitly supported the wider trade union movement, a law was passed prohibiting their affiliation to the TUC and Labour Party. This was repealed in 1946, and today, with only a few significant exceptions, the major public sector unions are affiliated to the TUC. (Public employees comprise roughly half the membership of unions affiliated to the TUC, nearly 5 out of 10 million in 1972.) Along with a widespread development of union security agreements, TUC disputes machinery resolves many potential organisation problems arising from competitive multiunionism. Parts of the civil service, most notably the health services, still contain many staff associations and professional associations that operate alongside TUC-affiliated unions and occasionally come into conflict with them.

Affiliation to the Labour Party and the sponsoring of Members of Parliament is usual for most of the manual workers' unions in the public sector but rare for the nonmanual unions. However, various forms of political pressure group activities are common to all public sector unions, particularly on such matters as pensions, incomes policies, and structural reorganisation of the services that are not amenable to direct negotiation. Recently, the most dramatic form of pressure group activity—the political strike and demonstration—has developed on a small but unprecedented scale in Britain, and public sector unions in the civil service and teaching sectors have come to the forefront.

Collective bargaining

The British system of industrial relations has been characterised by a clear preference for collective bargaining over other methods of wage determination in both the public and private sector. However, the term collective bargaining is applied to widely divergent processes and machinery, with variations in the level at which negotiations take place, the units of application, the form and content of agreements, and criteria customarily emphasised by the parties. Some of these differences will be explored and later the problem of government interference in the process will be examined.

The recognition of unions and employee associations by an employing authority for the purposes of bargaining or consultation has been subject to virtually no legal regulation in Britain until 1971; it has been at the discretion of the employer, although influenced by union pressure. There is a legal duty for the boards of nationalised industries to seek consultation and bargaining arrangements with employee organisations that are "appropriate" (parallel, although different, obligations exist with respect to teachers) but no statutory criteria are laid down to limit the discretion of employing authorities in fulfilling such a duty.[4] In practice, this has resulted in more or less overt collusion between employees and long-recognised unions to prevent aspiring bargaining agents (often staff associations or embryonic breakaway unions) from obtaining recognition. This has been more noticeable in the public than private sector, partly because of the typically larger and more heterogeneous bargaining units. The first year's operation of the Industrial Relations Act suggests that the new legal procedures for attempting to obtain recognition may not seriously disturb this situation.[5]

The level at which negotiation takes place for most public sector collective bargaining is the national or industry-wide level in contrast to the decentralisation of much negotiation in manufacturing industries in recent years. For most nonmanual workers, and many manual workers in the public sector, uniformity of pay and conditions is emphasised rather than flexible conditions negotiated locally. This tendency has been questioned in recent years by all parties concerned with manual workers. Trade unions have reacted against the limited opportunities for increasing earnings at workplace level via incentive schemes, special allowances, etc., while some public sector managers and various investigative public agencies—most notably the National Board for Prices and Incomes (NBPI 1965–70)—have recommended local productivity or incentive schemes to improve manpower utilisation. In local authorities, the health service and electricity supply industry, low pay and low productivity have been identified as related problems that can only be solved by more decentralised bargaining. Success has been limited, so far, by the relative organisational weaknesses and inadequate skills of local level union and management representatives in dealing with work measurement and cost-control mechanisms.

The form of collective agreements In the public sector, as in private manufacturing industries, is characterised by the absence of direct legal enforcement between the parties. The decisions of negotiating committees can be viewed as recommendations to executive authorities rather than as legal contracts, but they have legal consequences; for example, they become implied terms in the contract of employment between an individual employee and his employing authority (in the nationalised industries and local government) or embodied in statutory orders made by government ministers (health service, police, teachers). In addition, under section 8 of the Terms and Conditions of Employment Act 1959, unions may appeal to a permanent Industrial Arbitration Board (previously, the Industrial Court) if employers do not implement the terms and conditions negotiated for that sector or industry. This is a typically British indirect means of enforcement compared with the legislative extension of negotiated terms found in several other countries. Generally speaking, the agreements made in the public sector are more precise, detailed, and formal than in most private industry bargaining. Invariably, they are fixed-term agreements rather than open-ended as in many other sectors.

The scope or content of agreements made in the public sector is limited by the typically national level of negotiation, but tends to be wider than many private agreements negotiated at this level. As might be expected from the above discussion, legislative enactment has played no part in excluding matters from the machinery of negotiation or consultation, except in the case of the police. The content of agreements has expanded over the years in response to trade union pressure, some managerial conception of the "model employer" obligations inherent in public sector employment, and changing social and economic circumstances and expectations. In concrete terms, public sector workers have generally enjoyed greater security of employment and better pensions than private sector workers. The former have been threatened by massive reductions in manpower in some of the nationalised industries (coal, railways and, currently, gas and steel) but even in these cases, much better than average procedural and substantive terms covering redundancies have usually been negotiated. Some parts of the public sector have also pioneered collective agreements that harmonised conditions for manual and nonmanual workers (electricity supply) and male and female workers (civil service) in the absence, until recently, of any legislation.

The criteria or principles used in determining pay and conditions in the public sector is an area that currently causes much concern. Traditionally, "comparability" with similar work or occupations in the private sector has been the overriding criterion for pay settlements. This principle finds its institutional apotheosis in the machinery that covers the pay of nonindustrial civil servants.

Since 1956, an independent Civil Service Pay Research Unit has carried out intensive investigations into the pay and conditions of comparable jobs in outside employment for each group of civil servants. The Research Unit then reports the results of its survey to the parties involved in negotiation who then attempt to reach agreement on the basis of this information and the secondary principle of internal relativities. Thus, the sensitive issues of which jobs are comparable and what pay and conditions exist for them, typical of most negotiations in Britain that are influenced by the comparability principle, are decided by an independent unit before negotiations begin. As the Research Unit's survey covers only half of the civil service occupations each year, a Central Pay Settlement based on price and wage movements is negotiated in alternative years. This machinery does not cover manual workers in the industrial civil service nor the pay of the highest civil servants whose pay is based on the recommendations of the Top Salaries Review Body.

The comparability principle seems to embody a number of advantages in facing up to the particular problems of public sector pay determination: it has an ethical justification in terms of its "fairness;" it takes account of labour market fluctuations; it operates whether or not work output can be measured satisfactorily, and it seems to preclude political interference. For these reasons, it has remained the most important argument in negotiations in the public sector, although in the last decade, it has been subjected to increasing criticism by governments and employing authorities.

First, the superficial "fairness" of comparability arguments loses much of its force when pay is isolated from other elements of the work-reward relationship, as often happens (with the exception of the civil service procedures). As public sector pay is negotiated primarily at a national level, little regard can be paid to differences in working conditions, skills, technological developments, and local labour market conditions. Second, the efficiency of most manual workers can be measured and, in recent years, enormous variations in labour utilisation and manning levels in different parts of the public sector have been revealed. Changes in working practices that impede efficiency cannot be expected without some extra reward, thus adding a productivity principle in pay determination and requiring a second, lower level of negotiation. Third, the principle of "ability to pay" is clearly applicable to parts of the public sector, most obviously in the nationalised industries. As the National Coal Board states in its 1971–72 report: "In replying to a claim of such magnitude, the Board could base their offer only on their commercial position (their ability to pay and the effect on the market of a price increase to pay for a high wages settlement) and on their financial objectives as laid down by successive Governments."[6] As indicated, ability to pay is greatly influenced by political decisions outside the control of the executive boards of public corporations, but it is an inevitable part of pay negotiations. For the central and local government sectors, ability to pay might be translated as "political embarrassment in paying" as wage increases are financed from central or local taxes. Finally, the traditional methods of pay determination have not provided immunity from political and government interference, and it is to this crucial problem that we must now turn.

Incomes policies and the public sector

Experience over the last 15 years has proved conclusively that any government policies to restrain wages will be applied more effectively in the public sector than elsewhere. Clearly, if a government decides that wage restraint is desirable in the interest of national economic policy, it is not surprising that it should apply such restraint to the pay of its own direct or indirect employees. The crucial issues seem to be whether this restraint occurs in the context of a national incomes policy, the precise mechanisms of intervention, as well as the response that can be expected from the public employees and their unions.

The evidence shows that no government has yet succeeded in

developing an incomes policy that has not discriminated against public employees. The various phases of the Labour Government's policy from 1965–69 seemed most likely to overcome this problem; norms for pay increases, criteria for exceptional cases, and an independent investigative body (NBPI) were established. In practice, the incomes policy machinery had more impact on the public sector than on private manufacturing industries and services. This occurred partly because of the choice of references to the NBPI; those on the pay scale of senior executives in the civil service, local governments, and nationalised industries, and the price references on the latter, indicate an attempt to pass over politically difficult decisions to an independent agency.

More important, it seems clear than any incomes policy machinery would have more impact on the public sector because of the visibility, size, and nature of the central negotiations that take place. Although there is no conclusive evidence that public sector pay settlements are "pattern-setting" in any discernible wage round, they are well-publicised because of the size of bargaining units involved. (More than 30 public sector agreements cover more than 20,000 employees, 18 cover more than 100,000, and 8 more than 200,000 employees.) In addition, pay rates comprise a much larger proportion of actual earnings for most public sector employees, compared with the earnings-drift in many manufacturing industries, and thus, are more amenable to administrative scrutiny and control.[7]

If public employees and their unions became disillusioned with the incomes policy of 1965–69, they have responded with more unease and bitterness since the election of the present government in June 1970. The government immediately abandoned any formal incomes policy machinery as part of its policy of disengagement from industry but, faced with a serious problem of inflation, attempted to reduce public sector pay settlements in the hope that private industry employers would do likewise. The government consistently denied direct intervention in pay negotiations, but widely publicised its opinion about the fairness of offers made by the employing authorities and stated that successive pay settlements should be reduced. This policy, known as the "invisible incomes policy," soon ran into trouble.

First, it became clear that the individual merits of union wages claims were regarded as subordinate to their position in the wage round, effectively undermining the idea of meaningful negotiations. Second, the government prevented the conciliation and arbitration services of the Department of Employment from being used during public sector disputes if it appeared that this might involve any increased offer by the employers, thus removing the most important means of dispute resolution. Third, the government policy depended on the support of public sector executives in particular and of public opinion in general. The former could be largely obtained via indirect financial mechanisms, although at the expense of personal and political difficulties between the government and public sector executives; but public opinion never clearly supported the government against the groups of workers involved in a conflict with it. In the absence of any policy of wage restraint applied throughout industry, public employees could easily demonstrate that they had been isolated for discriminatory treatment and gain considerable public support when they clearly were seen as low-paid workers engaged in providing essential public services.

Primarily for the above reasons, the first two years of the present government saw a series of very large confrontations with public sector unions. National strike action occurred in the postal service, local authorities, and coalmining industry and widespread disruption was caused by the industrial actions of electricity supply and railway workers. In these conflicts involving more than 1.5 million workers, the public was greatly inconvenienced, yet the government rarely seemed to win the battle for public opinion and support. In all except the postal workers' dispute, industrial action succeeded in winning exceptionally large settlements and while the government undoubtedly reduced pay awards elsewhere in the public sector, its setbacks, which culminated in the traumatic coalmining strike in the spring of 1972, necessitated a complete reversal of policy.

Talks between unions, management, and government failed to generate an acceptable voluntary prices and incomes policy and the subsequent statutory policy (a wage and price freeze followed by legally-backed periods of restraint) continues to provide serious problems for the public sector. In the first few months of 1973, gas workers, ancillary workers in the health service, London teachers, and civil servants have been engaged in various forms of industrial action. Although the industrial action failed to increase pay settlements above the statutory limits, it indicated the continuing dissatisfaction of public employees with what they consider to be unfair treatment, best exemplified by the case of civil servants. Under the system of "fair comparisons" and the machinery of Pay Research described above, civil servants should have received a pay increase on January 1, 1973, based on the wage increases in other sectors over the last two years. This process of "catching up" was first delayed, since no pay increases were allowed until the end of the freeze on April 1. Second, the size of the delayed increase was drastically reduced; it should have reflected the high level of pay settlements prior to the freeze to conform with the statutory limits that applied until autumn 1973. I must be stressed that the industrial action by civil servants, health workers, gas workers, and the other groups mentioned earlier was virtually unprecedented in the British public sector.

Attempts by some public sector unions to develop more sustained and effective coordination to prevent the government from isolating or "picking off" individual groups have not produced any notable results as yet. It has been suggested that public sector pay claims should be coordinated in timing, a common policy should be adopted on certain bargaining issues, and the idea of one claim for all public sector workers directed at the government, not the employing authority, has been aired. This discussion within the TUC has advanced no further than the wider issue of TUC authority and power vis-a-vis the autonomy of individual affiliated unions. Public sector unions are divided and their sectional interests will prevent any far-reaching attempts at policy coordination.

In Britain, there is no constitutional guarantee of the "right to strike" and in the law there are no important differences between public and private employee rights or immunities from legal action during the course of strikes. The criminal liabilities that some public sector workers may incur (police, postmen and public utility workers) have rarely been used. The 1971 Industrial Relations Act alters the legal parameters of industrial action in many and complex ways, but the one area most likely to affect public sector strikes concerns the provision of procedures that the government may invoke during strikes that precipitate national emergencies. The "cooling-off procedure (similar to the U.S. legislation) and compulsory strike ballots were used in the railway dispute last year without notable success, but national disputes are more likely to give rise to "national emergencies" than private sector strikes because of the nature of the services provided by many parts of the public sector.

Voluntary arbitration procedures form the last stage of disputes procedures in most parts of the public sector and have traditionally been viewed as more effective than industrial action for resolving conflicts. Distinctions are rarely made between "disputes of interest" and "disputes of rights" in these procedures, although some issues are excluded from the jurisdiction of most of the tribunals. In both the coalmining and railway disputes, the unions refused to submit their claims to the arbitration tribunals, indicating their diminishing confidence in the impartiality of independent chairmen at a time of government public sector pay restraint. This unease was also manifested in the civil service when the government refused to reappoint the independent chairman after he had been associated with a settlement they believed to be against "the national interest" in an independent enquiry into a dispute affecting local government workers.

Consultation and participation

As might be expected, the nationalised industries have been the focus of most discussion relating to the participation of workers in the operation of the public sector. Much of the debate that preceded the Nationalisation Acts of 1945–49, centred on the desirability of direct worker/union representation on the boards of public corporations. It was finally decided that professional managers should be selected solely on the basis of "their competence to administer the industry" and that if any union leader should satisfy such a requirement, he would have to relinquish his union position on appointment. This was viewed as a guarantee of union independence that might be compromised by involvement in corporation policy decisions. Collective bargaining and multilevel joint consultation were seen as the most effective vehicles of worker participation, as is the case in the rest of the public sector and private industry.

This situation has not changed fundamentally, but some interest has been aroused by the experiment of employee-directors in the steel industry. Since 1968, the divisional boards of the Steel Corporation have included a few employee-directors. These employees, who continue to spend about half their working time in their normal jobs, are expected to act as an extra means of communication between the shop floor and the divisional board. They are appointed for four-year periods by a complex process involving workplace, union, and management nomination and selection. Experience so far indicates that all parties wish the experiment to become a permanent feature of the steel industry organisation, although they recognise the inevitably limited nature of the exercise. In an industry employing over 200,000 employees and engaged in a radical rationalisation program resulting in severe job insecurity in traditional steel-making areas, every means of increased participation should be welcomed, yet is likely to prove inadequate. Current developments in the European Economic Community (EEC) may well encourage more discussion about institutional arrangements for worker participation in management, but it seems unlikely that this will arouse much enthusiasm or far-reaching developments in the near future. The primacy of collective bargaining and direct political lobbying as the chosen union methods of pursuing their objectives remains a characteristic British approach.

Conclusions

Labour relations in the public sector seemed, until recently, to be far more stable and satisfactory than in the private sector of employment. If the machinery for negotiation, consultation, and arbitration was somewhat formalised, cumbersome, and centralised, this did not seem to worry the parties unduly. Unions and their leadership, especially those covering nonmanual workers, evolved to reflect the organisational structure of the sectors in which their members were employed. Until 20 years ago, the public sector seemed to provide more attractive and secure employment than most parts of private industry, so the moderation of union leaders was not questioned.

The post-war period of high employment and almost permanent wage inflation has altered this situation, although only in the past few years has this become dramatically apparent. It is now clear that government interference in collective bargaining is likely to remain a permanent part of any government's economic policies and that it can be applied most directly on the public sector. This challenges the whole apparatus of public sector negotiating machinery and ingrained union belief in "free collective bargaining." In recent months, the current pay policy seems to have totally undermined the functions of national union negotiators; they have been unable to bargain or submit their claims to arbitration or committees of inquiry or do anything else except reluctantly lead their members in industrial actions with little hope of success. Unrest in the public sector has been widespread; union leaders typically respond to pressure from members with no previous experience of industrial militancy. This has radically altered the pattern of industrial conflict in Britain; lengthy official disputes have occurred in the public sector and overshadowed what was believed to be the "English disease"—short, wildcat strikes in manufacturing industries.

Recent unrest can also be traced to the major structural and organisational changes that are occurring in almost every part of the public sector. Typically this has involved seemingly endless discussions about the need to change structures often half-a-century old, followed by widespread dislocation as traditional machinery is exposed to new organisational demands. This may provoke more similarity with private sector institutions as the direction of change indicates the need for greater flexibility and decentralisation in industrial relations practices. Finally, the

1971 Industrial Relations Act, by providing a comprehensive framework of collective labour law for public and private employment, would appear at first to encourage more similarity between the sectors and a more legalistic approach in British labour relations. The evidence so far, however limited, suggests that its impact may remain minimal outside the area of unfair dismissals. Serious amendment or wholesale repeal are, in any event, likely and the tradition of voluntarism seems relatively undisturbed by the Act's frontal assault.

1. The public sector was largely exempted from the criticisms made by the *Royal Commission on Trade Unions and Employers' Associations*, HMSO, London.
2. Raymond Loveridge, *Collective Bargaining by National Employees in the United Kingdom* (Ann Arbor: Institute of Labor and Industrial Relations, 1971), pp. 68-76.
3. G. Reid and K. Allen, *Nationalised Industries* (London: Penguin, 1970).
4. B. A. Hepple and Paul O'Higgins, *Public Employee Trade Unionism in the United Kingdom: The Legal Framework*, (Ann Arbor: Institute of Labor and Industrial Relations, 1971).
5. The most important case so far concerns the failure of the Telecommunications Staff Association to gain recognition in the Post Office.
6. *NCB Report and Accounts 1971-72, Vol. 1. Report*, HMSO, London.
7. For a more detailed discussion of the role of the National Board for Prices and Incomes and its impact on the public sector, see the article by R. J. Liddle and W. E. J. McCarthy in the *British Journal of Industrial Relations*, November 1972.

5

Labour Relations in the Public Sector in France

*Jean-Maurice Verdier**

*Professor, Paris University X (Paris-Nanterre).

A LTHOUGH it has been subjected to very little detailed and systematic scrutiny, the question of labour relations in the French public sector is one of great interest in view of the considerable proportions this sector has assumed, especially since the large-scale nationalisations that followed the Liberation. While labour relations in the public sector have many important characteristics that set them apart, nevertheless they undeniably affect labour relations in the private sector and are in turn affected by them.

This chapter will be limited to a discussion of the principal features of labour relations in the public sector in France, and will in particular endeavour to explain the main and highly significant trend of recent years: the emergence and continuous development of collective bargaining in a sector from which it was once virtually excluded. The first part of the chapter will accordingly be devoted to a description of the legal framework governing labour relations in the public sector, and the second part to an explanation of why and how collective bargaining has developed in that sector.

Legal framework of labour relations in the public sector

Although the public sector in France is highly diversified, the branches that compose it share a number of common features with regard to labour relations. The same diversity and resemblances are to be found in the machinery providing for workers' participation in management in these different branches.

Diversity

Occupying as it does a very prominent place in the economy and as an employer (it accounts for nearly 3 million workers, or some 20 percent of all wage and salary earners in France), the public sector is characterised by great diversity as regards the legal framework of labour relations.

(1) The *civil service* must be treated as a thing apart, since its members are subject to the special regulations (or "statutes") for civil servants, which are highly authoritarian, lay great emphasis on hierarchy, and fall outside the normal rules of labour legislation. The civil service comprises the staffs of the large state administrations at the national, regional, departmental and local levels.

(2) On the other hand, the rules of labour law apply in principle to the staffs of the *public undertakings,* but even here certain distinctions must be made. Although it is not necessary to consider here whether these undertakings are entirely state-owned (large nationalised banks, nationalised insurance companies, French Electricity and Gas Board (EGF), French National Coal Board) or only partly so, as in the case of "mixed economy" companies such as the French National Railways (SNCF) or Air France, on the other hand it is very important to realise that in some of these very large undertakings, the staff regulations, which are generally established by statutory provision but sometimes by joint agreement, differ in many respects

from the prevailing social legislation as reflected in ordinary law. This is true, for example, of the SNCF, the EGF, the French National Coal Board and the Divisional Coalfields (miners' statutes), to mention only a few.

(3) Account must also be taken of the fact that although most of the public undertakings are industrial and commercial concerns and are accordingly subject, as to their administration, to commercial law, and as to staff relations, to labour law, there are other undertakings which do not fall into this category and whose staff are frequently subject to highly individual rules, the specific provisions of which depend on the nature of their operations (e.g. undertakings engaged on national defence work).

(4) Finally, a distinction must also be made between public undertakings that provide services to the public and those that do not. Thus, a public undertaking such as the Renault Works, which were nationalised in 1945 for purely political reasons, does not provide a public service in the usual sense of the term and is therefore in principle on exactly the same footing as a private undertaking as regards its management and its staff relations. It is true that Renault acts as a pace-setter, not only for the economy (and particularly the export industry) but above all as regards conditions of work and social benefits; since 1955 a series of agreements between Renault's management and the unions have blazed the way for important legislative reforms (especially in the field of holidays with pay). Renault workers, however, are not subject to certain restrictive rules applying to public service workers, such as the ban imposed on wildcat or staggered strikes by the Act of 31 July 1963, or certain limitations on the right to strike affecting particular categories of public servants (policemen, magistrates, prison staff, air traffic controllers, etc.).

Naturally, this discrimination in law frequently has a very great influence on labour relations. In particular, it affects the machinery for worker participation (see below) and collective bargaining. The laws governing collective labour agreements (Acts of 1950 and 1971) do not apply to undertakings whose staff are covered by "statutes"; however, it will be shown in the second part of this chapter that in recent years this has not prevented the development of collective bargaining in undertakings of this kind.

Resemblances

The differences just alluded to must not blind one to the features the various branches have in common, which are equally relevant to an understanding of labour relations in the public sector.

In the first place, it should be pointed out that notwithstanding their differing legal status, the vast majority of public employees, who are not classed as officials and are therefore not subject to the regulations applying to civil servants, are covered by the ordinary labour laws. Moreover, even in the civil service there has latterly been a growing tendency to recruit part of the staff on temporary contracts, owing to the lack of sufficient established posts, and such temporary public servants are also subject to these laws.

Above all, it should not be forgotten that the right to organise and to bargain collectively has been recognised as generally applicable in France since the adoption of the 1946 Constitution, and that this right is consequently enjoyed by public officials no less than by public employees. Exceptions are rare (office-holders in ministries, legal officers, heads of banking and financial establishments). Although some limitations are placed on the right to organise in the civil service, officials can nevertheless exercise that right in its essentials. It follows that trade unions of civil servants and public employees are not only lawful but numerous, strong and of long standing, and it is noteworthy that the level of trade union membership, which is rather low in France as a whole (20 to 25 per cent), is particularly high in the public undertakings and administrations. While, as in the private sector, this level is liable to vary greatly from one industry or undertaking to another, there are a good many public undertakings in which it is as high as 80 or 90 percent.

Generally speaking, the trade unions of civil servants or employees in the public undertakings are affiliated to one or other of the large trade union confederations—the General Confederation of Labour (CGT), the French Democratic Confederation of Labour (CFDT), the General Confederation of Labour-*Force Ouvrière* (CGT-FO), the French Confederation of Christian Workers (CFTC), or the General Confederation of Executive Staffs (CGC) —although they may constitute relatively independent national unions within these confederations (e.g. railway workers', electricity and gas workers', miners' unions). On the managment side, it must be noted that some administrations (e.g. the EGF, the SNCF, the French National Coal Board) are unable to join an employers' association for the simple reason that their undertaking constitutes the entire indusutry. On the other hand, some administrations are affiliated to employers' organisations in their sector; thus the Renault Works are affiliated to the Union of Metal and Mining Industries (UIMM), while the heads of the large nationalised banks belong to the Professional Association for the Banking Trade (APB) —membership of which is in fact compulsory and which is not an employers' association in the usual sense.

In any event, the special nature of the public undertakings and administrations means that negotiations take place not between employers' and workers' organisations, but between the latter, on the one hand, and, on the other, either the management of the undertaking, the minister responsible for the administration concerned or the minister responsible for the public service.

Participation

Trade unions representing workers in public undertakings or officials are associated to a variable extent in the management of the undertakings or in the operation of the administration. However, a distinction must also be made in this connection between the civil service on the one hand and the public undertakings on the other.

Unions of officials in the civil service enjoy to some extent the right to be represented in the hierarchic authority and to participate in the management of the service and in decisions on disciplinary matters. Half of the membership of the Higher Council for the Civil Service (CSFP) and of the joint technical committees consist of staff representatives, nominated on the proposal of the representative trade unions in the case of the Council, and directly by the unions in that of the committees. It should nevertheless be observed that the role of the Council and the joint technical committees is essentially advisory.

The case of the public undertakings deserves closer study, however; it is complicated by the existence in some of these enterprises, just as in private undertakings, of shop stewards and work committees, elected in both cases by the employees; the former are primarily concerned with bread and butter issues, the latter with advising on the economic and social management of the undertaking and on the administration of its welfare services. Generally speaking, however, the trade unions themselves have a role to play both in the bodies responsible for managing the undertaking and in the bodies specialising in personnel problems.

Management of Undertakings

One of the fundamental aims of the nationalisation drive that was carried through in France after the Liberation was to associate representatives of the State, the customers and the staff in the management of the large credit, insurance, rail and air transport, and power production and distribution concerns that were taken into public ownership. Thus—without attempting here to go into details, which vary from one public undertaking to another—tripartite co-management is achieved at the level of the board of management of each such undertaking, the workers' representatives occupying one-third of the seats on these boards.

While the most representative trade unions always have a say in the appointment of the workers' members, the method of appointment varies. Sometimes it is made directly by the unions (as in the boards of management of the Divisional Coalfields or of the EGF distribution services), sometimes the unions suggest names to the responsible minister, who has the power of decision but can choose only between the names proposed (national electricity and gas services, French National Coal Board), and sometimes the unions only intervene indirectly through a specialised body (thus it is the works committee which appoints representatives in the Renault Works, or submits proposals to the minister in the Gnôme et Rhône Works); in such situations, trade union participation exists only to the extent that the unions are represented on the works committees, but in practice this is always the case.

In order to give a more accurate picture of trade union participation in the management bodies of public undertakings, it should be added that over and above the workers' representatives just alluded to, the boards of management sometimes also include representatives of the unions themselves (as for instance in the case of the nationalised banks and the French National Coal Board).

Personnel Problems

Bodies specialised in dealing with personnel problems also exist, only one example of which will be cited. The national statutes for the staff of the electricity and gas industries provide for the establishment of various personnel boards, namely a higher national board, inter-regional boards and secondary boards (in each operational unit or service), composed in equal numbers of representatives of management and of the staff, the latter being appointed by the Minister for Industry, but on the proposal of the most representative trade unions. The staff representatives on the joint production committees, who also account for 50 percent of the membership, are elected by the staff. Although the unions can put up candidates, independent candidates could in theory win every seat; in practice, however, the high level of unionisation in these industries ensures that the unions enjoy a near-monopoly.

Similar systems, characterised by the same diversity, operate in the SNCF and the French National Coal Board. Account must, however, be taken of the existence of various boards, committees or working groups established by agreements between the managements and the unions, on which the latter have representatives appointed directly by them. The railways provide a significant example of this. Since the beginning of 1968, the problems and wide-ranging social implications raised by the operational modernisation of rail transport have prompted the General Manager of the SNCF to hold frequent personal meetings with representatives of the large railwaymen's unions. Both sides point to the considerable amount of work done at these "round-table, meetings on the social consequences of modernisation, thanks to which relations between management and workers have substantially improved. If one also takes into consideration the numerous statutory bodies which meet regularly at the local level, altogether over 9,000 persons, most, if not all, of whom are active trade unionists, are involved in frequent meetings. This is some measure of the extent of the dialogue that has been instituted between management and union representatives.

Extent of Independent Decision Making

Clearly, therefore, by its very nature, the system of tripartite management (State, customers and staff) enables the trade unions to have a say in the decisions made. Equally clearly, however, this participation is meaningful only to the extent that managerial decision-making power is effective at the local level.

It has become a commonplace to note, as the rapporteur of the Interministerial Committee for Public Undertakings has done, that the nationalised undertakings have been used directly and freely by the authorities to promote their general policies. To do this, the authorities have availed themselves of the machinery and powers provided for in the general statutes of public undertakings. On the one hand, there are the bodies responsible for inspection and control; these may be of general scope, as in the case of the Auditing Board for Public Undertakings or the State Audit Office, or they may be limited to a particular undertaking, as in the case of the government commissioners or officials responsible for economic and financial control. And on the other hand, there is the fact that the supervising authority, in other words the Government, has the power to approve or veto the most important decisions. Moreover, the authorities have a say, one way or another, in the choice of the general manager. Thus it is not surprising that in practice the major decisions are taken by the Government itself, especially in very large undertakings such as the French Electricity Board, the mines or the SNCF, and that the state-owned undertakings should not enjoy any real independence save in respect of routine administration, with the Government acting as watchdog even there. The trade unions have protested against this excessive supervision, which in their view is concentrated too much on financial and not enough on economical aspects; as soon as they realised they no longer had any influence over the policies of the undertakings, their initial eagerness to co-operate waned and they began to concentrate their energies increasingly on securing better wages and working conditions. Indeed, even when decisions can be taken in a climate of real independence, as in the deliberations of boards of management on questions of general policy, the unions have often been systematically outvoted and thus relegated to a role of opposition; and in day-to-day management the influence of the unions has for the most part been limited, save in the field of social questions.

Although it is hardly to be expected that the managements of public undertakings should be given a completely free hand in matters directly affecting the general interest (e.g. decisions on investments or output levels), the need has been felt to let them manage their everyday affairs without external interference. In fact it was this need for greater independence, in particular, that led to the moves for the reform of public undertakings which are currently under consideration and have already been introduced in the SNCF. Only experience can show whether trade union participation in management will be reinforced by these measures. In the changed over-all climate brought about by official encouragement for the conclusion of collective agreements between managements and unions, however, negotiations are already taking place almost continuously over their substantive provisions and implementation, leading in practice to increased participation by the unions, albeit still in an essentially advisory capacity.

Development of collective bargaining

This is indisputably one of the most striking modern trends in French industrial relations, particularly since the crisis of May-June 1968. It is not, of course, entirely new. The statutes of many large public undertakings already contained provision for collective bargaining. In the case of SNCF, for example, provision was made for the trade unions to have a hand, within the tripartite joint committee on the statutes, in drafting or amending the many different regulations governing the conditions of employment and career service of employees. Joint committees for the various regions or establishments—on which the unions are also represented—are responsible for adapting these regulations to the different services and for enforcing them. Thus the unions already had some influence on conditions of work, although the statutory requirement that the decisions of the joint committee be approved by the competent minister meant that in fact the Government had the last word. Nevertheless, the foundations for permanent bargaining had already been laid, which was more than could be said for the civil service, even if, as the authorities had the final say, negotiated settlements were not automatically implemented.

This privileged situation, to which the relative job security and various other substantial advantages enjoyed by workers in the public sector also contributed, was soon undermined by increasing state interference reflected partly in the loss of managerial independence and partly in the intensified controls already mentioned. Earnings had fallen well behind those in the private sector, and the Government had failed to keep some of its promises. In a report submitted over ten years ago by the Counsellor of State, Mr. Toutée, the deterioration in the social climate was described as follows: "Although they express themselves with varying degrees of emphasis, the trade union representatives are virtually unanimous in considering that, in the matter of remuneration, the story of their relations with the authorities is one of patience exhausted, of trust misplaced, of agreements unfulfilled and of promises unkept; their attitude ranges from sheer lassitude to bitterness and even indignation."

Not surprisingly, therefore, workers in the public sector tried to win back the ground they had lost by resorting to the strike weapon. This explains the large-scale outbreak of strikes in the nationalised sector: in 1961, for example, nationalised undertakings accounted for 55 percent of the working days lost in France through strikes although they employed only 6 percent of all French workers.

It is the growing awareness of this exceptionally tense situation which has prompted the new developments that have been noted latterly. These have been, on the one hand, a widening range of issues regarded as negotiable, and on the other hand, and in particular, the theoretical and practical progress made towards genuine bargaining, that is to say, bargaining aimed at producing agreements binding on both parties. One of the chief results of this process has been the emergence of wage bargaining.

Genuine bargaining

The first point to be noted is that a bargaining process worthy of the name has been established in a sector from which it had previously been excluded, just as in the civil service, because the State (which was at the same time the employer) insisted on exercising its sovereign authority. The opinions and personalities of certain political leaders appear in some cases to have helped substantially to bring about the change. This development can be seen objectively as reflecting the emergence of a crucial new factor—a desire to negotiate on the management side. It should be added, however, that this change of heart has taken place at two levels.

At the government level, in the first place, we find a wish to relinquish the power of direct control and to restore to managements of undertakings the independence of which they had been progressively stripped to the benefit of the supervising authorities—something which those responsible for the nationalisation of these undertakings had not intended. Reservations can be expressed as to the adequacy of the leeway now left to these managements; for example, the statutes of the SNCF provide that the decisions of the joint committee must always be approved by the supervising authority, and the latter can, of course, use its position to influence the outcome.

Next, at the level of the undertakings, the managements, having now been reinstated as valid bargaining partners as a result of their newly regained independence, are no longer in a position to shirk responsibility by hiding behind the skirts of the supervising authority. Yet this in itself would not have sufficed to start the bargaining process moving. Managements also had to come round to accepting trade unions as a fact of life, that is to say, to recognise them as a necessary partner in discussions, and to resolve to keep them honestly, regularly and completely informed of relevant developments.

A good example of such consultation is provided by the series of "round-table" meetings on the social consequences of modernisation in the French railways, to which reference was made earlier. Following talks that were held regularly in the first quarter of 1968, were interrupted in May of that year, were overshadowed by the talks that followed the Grenelle statement[1], and were resumed in June, these meetings finally led to the basic agreement of 11 July 1968 respecting the social implications of modernisation (retraining, additional promotions to compensate for reductions in staff, action to step up general and vocational training, adaptation of staff rules to changing staff functions, procedures for keeping trade unions and joint committees fully informed, etc.). The SNCF agreement of 4 June 1968, which followed the Grenelle statement, provided for the establishment of a tripartite board to examine general problems of transport policy. Thus a vast new area of discussion was added to the traditional scope of the statutes proper. While the field of negotiation reached its apogee with the initiation of talks on remuneration and salaries within the framework of the so-called "progress" agreements, an even more notable development was the institutionalisation of the bargaining process.

The introduction in 1965 of what was known as the "Toutée" procedure in four of the largest public undertakings (the EGF, the SNCF, the French National Coal Board and the Paris Independent Transport Authority (RATP)) had initiated the general institutionalisation of wage bargaining, since the trade unions participating in the first stage (annual calculation of the total wage bill for the past year) were consulted before the Government proceeded to fix the rate by which this wage bill could be increased during the following year (second stage), and they held negotiations with management as to how the increase should be shared out (third stage). Despite the loss of enthusiasm for this approach, which was confirmed by the Grenelle statement and explained by the lack of independence on the part of the managements and the ineffectiveness of the consultations, the positive aspects of a procedure providing for the joint assessment and analysis of the total wage bill nevertheless had something to recommend them.

Accordingly, at the end of 1968, ways and means of improving the procedure were studied and proposed in the Martin report, which recommended opening up broader opportunities—albeit still with limitations—of discussing the size of the total wage bill. Going a step further, however, the Government decided in September 1969 to refrain in future from fixing the annual rate of increase of the wage bill unilaterally, and to treat it instead as an item to be negotiated with the trade unions, along with the conclusion of agreements lasting several years and covering remuneration, conditions of work and guarantees for the efficient and uninterrupted operation of the services provided to the public. Despite difficulties due mainly to certain aspects of the policy of "progress" agreements (in particular, the "industrial peace" clauses), agreements were signed successively in the EGF (10 December 1969 and 9 February 1971), the SNCF (23 February 1970 and 11 January 1971), the French National Coal Board (2 March 1970), the Alsatian Potassium Mines (18 September 1970) and the RATP (13 October 1970). In 1971 and 1972 these agreements were extended or superseded by new ones.

Articulated bargaining

The second point worth noting is the development and general acceptance of what is known as "articulated" bargaining and of its most striking practical achievement to date: the introduction of wage bargaining in undertakings that, size for size, are comparable with whole industries in the private sector.

The wage agreement concluded in the EGF on 10 December 1969 fixed the rate of increase in the wage bill as a function both of the gross domestic product and of factors specific to the undertaking (output, size of labour force), the latter playing the less important part. But the agreement also laid down a wages policy: provision was made for a joint committee to calculate the increase in the total wage bill and distribute it in a way which would not only maintain the purchasing power of all employees but increase it, with the lowest-paid grades receiving proportionally larger increases.[2]

The other agreements of the same kind were designed, rather, to achieve a guaranteed increase in purchasing power over the year. For that purpose, they provided simultaneously for a phased increase in real wages at a rate (2 percent in the case of the French National Coal Board and the SNCF) taking account of the anticipated rise in the price index, and for an "escape clause" stipulating that, if prices were to go up faster than expected, wages would be further increased by the difference between the actual and the anticipated rise in the index. The addendum to the EGF's wage agreement signed on 9 February 1971 followed suit by guaranteeing a minimum increase in purchasing power of 2.5 percent.

In recent years the trade unions have demonstrated their ability to use collective bargaining to wring concessions from the employers. Thus in the EGF, the guaranteed rate of increase in puchasing power, after first being fixed at 2 percent, was raised to 2.5 percent; each year the working week has been shortened by one hour; and action has been initiated towards the extension of paid holidays, the revision of wage scales, and the improvement of pensions and various allowances. It is understandable that trade unions in other industries, such as coalmining, should have called for the negotiation of similar agreements, and that in 1972 they should have succeeded in securing salaried status for workers hitherto paid by the hour. Similarly, in the Alsatian Potassium Mines, after a bitter and protracted dispute the unions made a number of substantial gains, in particular an increase of 1.4 percent in the wage bill compared to the previous figure, and, for 1973, a 2 percent rise in purchasing power and a substantial increase in the year-end bonus, as well as a reduction of the working week to 40 hours with effect from 1974. For their part, employees of the SNCF also won substantial improvements for 1972 and 1973.

The agreements thus concluded call for two comments. On the one hand, above and beyond the achievement of wage bargaining, the trend is towards participation in decisions respecting wage policies themselves. Although at the moment such participation is confined to short-term agreements running for a year only, it has been introduced—and this is worth stressing—in undertakings comparable in scale with a major branch of industry in the private sector. On the other hand, bargaining is articulated, inasmuch as it covers a complete range of problems, even the most important ones (including jobs, careers, discipline, welfare services, hours and conditions of work, duty rosters, consequences of modernisation, allowances and compensation of all kinds, wages, etc.) ; one can only regret that in some areas (for example, the administration of welfare services in the SNCF) true bipartism has not been introduced, the trade unions being granted only minority representation. Bargaining is also articulated in the sense that it takes place at several levels, each problem being considered at the level at which it arises in practice. In the case of the SNCF, for example, questions relating to the statutes, modernisation and the determination of conditions of work are considered at the national level (through the joint committee, or the round-table discussions), while questions concerning the application of regulations provided for in the statutes, or the organisation of duty rosters, are discussed at local level (by working committees or joint works committees). It should be pointed out also that the conduct of bargaining on the articulated pattern has been greatly facilitated by the fact that trade union structures are closely modelled on those of the undertakings.

Permanent bargaining

A final consideration worth noting is that collective bargaining in the public undertakings is a practically continuous process. Bargaining appears to be conducted regularly, periodically, and according to a set—or at least planned—schedule. No doubt disputes are still numerous and strikes frequent; it is interesting in this connection that the authorities and the managements of public undertakings have decided not to insist that the trade unions undertake to refrain from striking, even during the limited life of the collective agreement. The fact remains that the application and renewal of the agreements, as well as their frequent improvement by successive addenda, require reasonably frequent and regular meetings. The trade unions readily acknowledge that the recent agreements or addenda thereto have been the outcome of real negotiations with managements which are not only willing to talk but also anxious to take advantage of the greater independence granted them by the Government to bargain at whatever level and on whatever subject appears likely to produce results. This analysis is confirmed by several aspects of the recent agreements.

In the first place, in the spirit of the agreements, frequent contacts are required merely to ensure their application. It is true that the commitment to observe "industrial peace" for the duration of the agreement, inserted in the 1969 EGF agreement, is not included in the other agreements, and was toned down in the addendum to the EGF agreement of 9 February 1971 to an undertaking "to meet to discuss any disagreement or dispute arising out of the operation of this instrument" and "to make every effort to settle the disagreement or dispute by negotiation"; but at least provision was thus made for contacts. More generally, the spirit of these agreements of limited duration—especially limited in the matter of wages (one year)—militates against their being denounced before they have expired (unless the situation should change dramatically) and in favour of joint examination of any difficulties experienced in applying them.

What is more, the contents of the agreements imply the need

for frequent, indeed periodical meetings in order to take note of changes in prices, wages, and the parameters used, and to draw the appropriate conclusions. Thus the collective agreement for the EGF makes a joint committee responsible for calculating and distributing the increase in the wage bill. Experience has even shown that the established timetable can be speeded up: the rise in prices having been greater than anticipated in 1969, the management and unions of the SNCF agreed to apply the escape clause with effect from October 1970 instead of 1 January 1971. Bringing forward the adjustment in this way was in conformity with the spirit if not the letter of the 1970 agreement and specific reference to this possibility is made in the addendum signed on 11 January 1971, provision being made for frequent meetings for this purpose.

Nor are wage questions the only ones to be affected in this way: changes in conditions of work led the parties to the addendum to make arrangements in 1971—pending submission of the question to the committee on the statutes—for the immediate establishment of a working group to study the improvement of these conditions in the services where they were least satisfactory.

Finally, this willingness to negotiate is accompanied by efforts on the part of managements to keep the trade unions and joint bodies regularly and fully informed. Sometimes managements are specifically required to provide information by the terms of the agreement, as in the case of the protocol of the SNCF on consultation and conciliation procedures for local or regional problems in the operational services, signed on 23 February 1970 and renewed for 1971 with a number of additional provisions.

Many more examples could be given showing that the idea of permanent bargaining is gaining widespread acceptance, backed by the assurance of regular information covering all problem areas. For the trade unions, this type of bargaining raises the difficult question of the preparation and training of the employees called upon to participate in it, while for the undertakings it implies the obligation to assist the unions to solve this question satisfactorily. Thus it cannot help but engender a new style of management-union relations.

It would be wrong to conclude without a reference to the stimulating effect on the private sector of successful bargaining in the public sector. The willingness of the Government and the managements of the large public undertakings to permit and assist in the establishment of true bargaining, for which the unions impatiently clamoured for so long; the institution of organised, articulated, and permanent bargaining; and lastly, the positive results obtained by this means, despite the difficulties encountered by some undertakings in their efforts to modernise their operations or reinforce their commercial position—all these achievements inevitably have an impact on other economic sectors as examples of what can be done. There is accordingly an obligation on the authorities to ensure that these efforts, which must spread and multiply, are duly pursued.

1. See Yves Delamotte: "Recent collective bargaining trends in France," in *International Labour Review*, April 1971, p. 359.
2. For further details see Delamotte, op. cit., pp. 367-368.

6

Labour Relations in the Public Sector of the Federal Republic of Germany: The Civil Servant's Role

*Thilo Ramm** *

A literal translation of the title of this chapter into German would inevitably surprise and confuse German lawyers because, in German legal terminology, the word "labour" is never applied to civil servants. The expression "labour relations" is applied only to *Arbeitnehmer,* not *Beamte.*

The distinction between *Arbeitnehmer* and *Beamte***

Arbeitnehmer are blue- and white-collar workers (and trainees), but *Beamte* are never considered to be *Arbeitnehmer* (see article 5, section 2, Labour Court Act).[1] *Beamte* have a special legal status. *Arbeitnehmer* and *Beamte* are subject to different laws; the *Arbeitnehmer* are covered by many labour statutes,

*Professor, University of Giessen.

**The German terms *Arbeitnehmer* and *Beamte* are difficult to translate. The former is a generic term covering all categories of workers and employees, white-collar as well as blue-collar. The second term refers specifically to public servants or civil servants. Details of the exact meaning of these terms under German law are explained in the body of this paper.

collective agreements (*Tarifvertraege*), work agreements (*Betriebsvereinbarungen*), and finally individual labour contracts (*Arbeitsvertraege*). Special statutes cover salaries, all working conditions, and social security provisions applying to the *Beamte*. Collective agreements for them do not exist.

The law covering blue- and white-collar workers (the only legislation referred to as "labour law") and the law covering *Beamte* are clearly distinct in Germany and are even considered to be of different legal natures; the former are covered by private and the latter by public law.[2] Therefore, labour-management conflicts are settled by different courts: the administrative courts have exclusive jurisdiction over *Beamte*[3] on all matters concerning salary, employment conditions, and social security; while the labour courts decide all disputes over salaries, wages, or working conditions dealing with the *Arbeitnehmer,* and the social courts have jurisdiction over their social security questions.

Private and public service

The distinction between *Beamte* and *Arbeitnehmer* does not correspond to the distinction between public and private service. Those terms reflect only who the employer is. Employees of a state, a community, or a proprietary industry are in public service; employees of a private corporation are in private service. In many cases the choice of terminology is arbitrary. Public utilities are sometimes private corporations and sometimes parts of the local or regional public administration. *Beamte,* as well as blue- and white-collar workers, may be employed in the public sector.[4] On the other hand, although it is exceptional, a *Beamter* can be employed in private service, e.g. a public enterprise, a savings-bank, or a municipal gas works may have changed its status to a private corporation while continuing to employ the *Beamte.*

The number of *Arbeitnehmer* in public service is higher than the number of *Beamte*: 825,000 blue-collar workers and 937,000 white-collar workers in contrast to 436,000 *Beamte.*[5] While the number of white-collar workers in the public sector exceeds that of manual workers, the opposite is true in the private sector. In the latter there are 11,372,000 manual workers and 7,200,000 white-collar workers.

The percentage of *Arbeitnehmer* compared to the percentage of *Beamte* employed in the public sector has increased considerably in this century. In 1913, for example, it stood at 88.8 percent *Beamte* to 11.2 percent white-collar *Arbeitnehmer* (blue-collar workers were not included in the statistics). By 1927, *Beamte* comprised 66.7 percent of the total public sector work force, white-collar workers, 13.5 percent and blue-collar employees 19.8 percent.[6] In 1971, the figures were *Beamte* 29.3 percent, white-collar workers 44.9 percent and blue-collar employees 25.8 percent. Moreover, during that time span the absolute number of *Beamte* remained relatively constant while the ranks of the white-collar *Arbeitnehmer* continued to swell. This shift made the latter an increasingly powerful group of employees within the public service.

No empirical study has been made describing which specific positions must be filled by white-collar *Arbeitnehmer* and which by *Beamte*. Generally speaking, however, the more important positions, especially those involved with governmental service, rather than with the management of public enterprises, are reserved for *Beamte*. In lesser positions, categories are even less clearly delineated and appear principally to reflect practices going back over many years. However, *Beamte* are in the majority in departments that deal with law and order—the police, military, and judiciary, for example. In addition, teachers, university professors and most postal and railroad employees are nearly all *Beamte*. On the other hand, white-collar workers are more prevalent in departments charged with administering the social security program or managing public utilities.

Regardless of the category to which they belong, employees in the public service (with the important exception of *Beamte* in leading positions) are subject to one common statute, the Federal Staff Representation Act (1955), a law similar to the Works Constitution Act of 1972 for private industry, although it provides a more modest form of codetermination. In addition to the federal statute, the states have their own staff representation acts, which follow the same pattern. The Works Council Act of 1920, which preceded the Works Constitution Acts of 1952 and 1972, permitted the government to decree that certain groups of *Beamte* or aspirants for such positions could be classified as blue- or white-collar workers under the meaning of that Act (section 13). This indicates that initially the Weimar Republic was attempting to eliminate the distinction between *Beamte* and other employees.

On one point the law is uniform for all employees in the public and private sectors: the right to organise is granted to everybody. Article 9, section 3, sentences 1 and 2 read as follows:

> The right to form combinations[7] to safeguard and improve working and economic conditions is guaranteed for everyone and for all occupations. Agreements that seek to restrict or impede this right are void; measures directed toward such purpose are illegal.

The *Beamtentum*

To understand the particular status of the *Beamte* and the present legal discussion *de lege ferenda* it is necessary to give a brief history of the development of the *Beamtentum*.[8] While labour law generally developed "from status to contract," the *Beamte* remained at the status stage. The basic structure of the *Beamtentum* was formed during the years of feudalism and absolute monarchy. The civil and military servant owed fidelity (*Treue*) to his prince, a special fidelity and obedience, as the Prussian General Code of 1794 put it. On the other hand, the prince looked after the *Beamte's* well-being (*Fuersorge*), which entailed not only his salary, but also full social benefits in case of sickness, disability or retirement, and pensions for his wife and other dependents. Therefore, the *Beamte* usually served, and still does so, for a "lifetime." The status he held influenced all aspects of his life, not only his job. To a large extent, this influence continues today.

This concept has survived the fall of the absolute and the succeeding constitutional monarchies (the specific German compromise between monarchy and parliamentarism during the 19th century) ; the breakdown of the Weimar Republic with the Reich President (who was actually characterized as a "substitute" emperor) ; and even the Nazi Reich Chancellor and Fuehrer system. While the *Beamtentum* has survived as an institution during all those years, it has, however, undergone some substantial changes.

The first change was the depersonalization of fidelity. This began with King Frederick the Great of Prussia, who considered himself to be the "first servant of the state." Consequently, the *Beamte* was seen as both a servant of the monarch and a servant of the state. When the state structure changed and the people, as represented by Parliament, were recognized as a power independent from the monarch and co-equal with him, the *Beamte* acquired still more independence. Since both monarch and Parliament had to agree to all statutes, the task of interpreting and implementing these statutes increasingly fell upon the courts and government administrators. "All administration is strictly bound to statute": This was the famous slogan circumscribing the foundation of the *Rechtsstaat* (rule of law) . Both judicial and executive power acquired independence from the monarch, and the concept of a nonpolitical, or neutral, *Beamtentum* was born. Nevertheless, while the theory had not been established, in practice the monarch (and the conservative nobility) still strongly influenced the appointments to managerial positions in government. Parliamentary control was, in fact, rather weak since neither the Reich Chancellor nor the cabinet were responsible to Parliament. Only gradually did the power to appoint and promote judges shift from the monarch to Parliament.

Constitutional monarchy liberated the *Beamte* from the arbitrary decisions of the monarch. Disciplinary courts and disciplinary legislation protected him against arbitrary dismissals or other sanctions. Claims for salary could be brought before the civil court and the entire service was divided into different types of career ladders (*Laufbahnen*) . Promotions were regulated mainly through seniority and qualifying examinations.

The tendency to exclude policy-making decisions as far as possible, one of the significant characteristics of the *Beamtentum,* was and is, of course, contradictory to the liberal ideology of efficiency and competition. In the context of German legal theory, state and society were considered to be two separate worlds. But in practice, the two worlds were very similar. German labour law was partially feudal. The German *Gesindeordnungen* for rural and domestic servants (Master and Servants Acts), which also obligated the servants to demonstrate fidelity to their employers and the employers, in turn, to show concern for the welfare of their employees, lasted until 1919 and had a common ideological basis with the law for *Beamte*. Even the labour relations of industrial workers were determined by paternalism. After less than 15 years, with the fall of the Weimar Republic in 1933, Nazism revived the earlier ideology of personal subordination and fidelity. The *Fuehrer* replaced the absolute monarch. But, again, this ideology was not restricted to the *Beamtentum*. It also covered labour relations in the private sector: The employer became the *Fuehrer* of the plant; his employees, the *Gefolgschaft,* owed him fidelity, while he owed paternalistic concern to them. The plant, in turn, was supervised and controlled from above as a cell of the *Volksgemeinschaft* (national community) .

This continuation of the old feudal tradition best explains why feudal thinking is still visible in German law and why labour lawyers still use the traditional terms "fidelity obligation" and "welfare obligation," considering them part of the individual labour contract. The spiritual links between present German labour law and the *Beamtentum* institution make it easy to understand the strong defense of this concept and its survival after the 1918 November revolution as well as after the fall of Nazism, despite the attempts of the Military Government after 1945 to abolish it. Under the Nazis, the "German *Beamte* Act" of 1937 consolidated these legal concepts. The old distinction between *Reichsbeamte,* state or other *Beamte* (as for instance of municipalities) , disappeared. With the fall of Nazism after 1945, the establishment of new states by the occupation forces led to the creation of state statutes for *Beamte.* Thereafter, the Federal Republic developed its own legislation governing *Beamte.* Today, federal legislation also provides a statutory framework for all state legislation governing *Beamte (Beamtenrechtsrahmen-gesetz* of 1957/1971), which reiterates the main provisions laid down in the Federal Act for *Beamte.* Federal legislation now governs salaries and social welfare provisions covering *Beamte.*

Nazism also destroyed the spiritual basis of the *Beamtentum.* The 1934 "Act to Restore Professional *Beamtentum*" abolished a guarantee hitherto considered fundamental, life-time employment. Jewish and politically "unreliable" *Beamte* were dismissed or pensioned, even though no charges had been brought against those individuals. Certainly, other *Beamte* profited by being promoted to fill the vacancies thus created and Nazis were appointed to *Beamte* positions. But the shock to the institution of *Beamtentum* remained. A second shock came with the denazification policy of the occupation forces; again the status of *Beamte* did not protect them against discharge, and the German Federal Constitutional Court upheld this decision.[9]

History tells us more about the present status of the German *Beamtentum* than does current law. The Bonn Basic Law says in article 33, section 4:

> The exercise of sovereign authority (*hoheitsrechtliche Befugnisse*) shall as a rule be assigned as a permanent duty to members of the public service who stand in a public law relationship of service and fidelity.

and in section 5:

> The law regarding public service shall be determined with due regard to the traditional principles of the professional *Beamtentum.*

What these traditional principles are, and whether or not they have been altered by recent interpretations have been left to the courts and to academic scholars (who traditionally exercise considerable influence on the courts and public legal opinion) to decide. Whether fundamental rights in Germany are the basis of all statutory law and therefore, take precedence over the principles that controlled the traditional operations of professional *Beamtentum* (the latter constantly subject to change) is a political question, a question of how strong liberalism is at any given moment in Germany. In practice, lawyers have leaned heavily on past history in interpreting the law. The institution of the *Beamtentum* was guaranteed by the 1919 Weimar Constitution at a time when the conservative parties were afraid that the Communists and Social Democrats would destroy the *Beamtentum* after the fall of the monarchy, since that institution represented the head and shield of the bureaucracy which Karl Marx and his followers had so solemnly condemned. Article 129 of the Weimar Constitution spelled out the basic features of the *Beamtentum*: normally, lifetime appointment; statutory regulation of pension rights and dependents' maintenance; inviolability of justly-acquired rights; enforceability of pecuniary claims; statutory provisions and procedures for suspension, retirement, or transfer to a position receiving a lesser salary; and remedies against any disciplinary sanctions. Article 130 of the Weimar Constitution also added, "The *Beamte* are servants of the community and not of a party. Freedom of political conviction and freedom of association is guaranteed to all *Beamte*."

These two articles of the Weimar Constitution are the foundation for three main developments: the erosion of the old tradition of special subordination of the *Beamte* to the state, a trend stemming from the growing influence of politics; the current dispute concerning the prohibition of strikes for all *Beamte;* and the equalization of the status of *Beamte* to that of other public employees.

The erosion of the special subordination of Beamte and the influence of politics

An individual achieves the status of *Beamte* when he is appointed to the position for which he has applied and received his document of appointment. Statutory provisions governing the duties of the *Beamte* differ essentially from the contractual obligations of other public employees. The special relationship of subordination (*besonderes Gewaltverhältnis*) [10] was considered to affect the whole person, even his private life. Until a decade ago, for instance, adultery was subject to disciplinary sanction; if found guilty, the *Beamter* was discharged. This rule has gradually disappeared, but there is still the rule that the behavior of the *Beamte* "inside and outside of service must be in accordance with the respect and the confidence required by his profession" (article 53, Federal *Beamte* Act). More and more, however, the demand that the *Beamte* serve as models of behavior has become an empty phrase.

Other problems, however, have remained unsolved. The first deals with the freedom of speech and political activities. The Federal *Beamte* Act says in article 53:

> The *Beamte* has to be as moderate and reserved in his political activities as is required by his position in the community and by the duties of his office.

Generally, all *Beamte,* soldiers and judges included, are permitted to be members of political parties and to participate in party activities. They may stand for election although, if elected, they must go on leave of absence. There is some question as to whether they may join radical parties or, more precisely, parties that "according to their aims or their behavior intend to prejudice or to abolish the liberal democratic basic order or to endanger the existence of the Federal Republic of Germany and therefore are prohibited" (article 9, section 2, Bonn Basic Law). The prohibition of a party requires a decision by the Federal Constitutional Court, but there is some dispute as to whether the government can take disciplinary action against *Beamte* involved in activities on behalf of a radical party in the absence of such a decision, or whether it may refuse the appointment of applicants for this reason alone. In practice, the argument revolves around members of the Communist Party or of the "New Left" movement, and the question is mainly important with regard to teachers. The courts have not yet decided in such cases.

Psychologically, the problem includes various aspects: the government's fear of communist underground activities; the naive assumption on the part of those who advocate drastic social change that they can do so without endangering their jobs or, to phrase it another way, that they can assume the role of revolutionaries while drawing a government salary; and the question of government monoply in the educational field. These are the most significant features that underlie the current political arguments.

Legal theory is clear and of long precedent. As indicated earlier, during the period of the Weimar Republic the first overt attempts were made to come to grips with the problem of a *Beamte's* permissible political activities. One could, of course, question whether the *Beamtentum* has, in fact, ever been truly apolitical or neutral or, indeed, if during the period of the monarchy the *Beamte* can be said to have been in sympathy with the mainstream of German thought. Certainly, at that time, the *Beamte* were conservatives devoted to the monarch, or they straddled the fence between conservatism and liberalism. During the Weimar Republic many *Beamte* became hostile or indifferent towards the new state. Thus, in 1922, a law was passed obligating the *Reich Beamte* to support the constitutional republican supreme power (*Staatsgewalt*). The present Federal law has extended this obligation.

> The *Beamte* must profess by his general behavior the liberal democratic basic order in the sense of the Basic Law and must profess support for its maintenance (article 52).

This was the basis for the declaration made by the German Prime Minister and Federal Chancellor on January 28, 1972, that membership in and support of parties hostile to the Constitution will normally be considered a conflict of loyalties and will entitle the "master" (*Dienstherr*) to intervene if necessary. Serious doubts concerning the loyalty of an applicant justify the refusal of his application.[11] This step was taken because the former stricture that a *Beamte* owed complete obedience to the statutes has increasingly been replaced by legal provisions granting him a wide sphere of discretion. As a consequence of the *Beamte's* greater independence and responsibility their personal reliability has assumed greater importance. However, the evaluation of personal reliability, especially if applicants are very young, is a very difficult task that can scarcely be fulfilled satisfactorily for a large number of persons. If the number of *Beamte* is not to be radically diminished, a practical solution can probably be found in delineating the special functions of the *Beamte,* and letting those serve as bases upon which their actions can be measured.

The problem mentioned above is just one aspect of the growing influence of politics on appointments and promotions of *Beamte*. Those appointed generally serve in their positions for the rest of their working lives and that in itself is sufficient reason for Parliament to try to obtain more influence over the choices made for the more important offices such as judgeships. At the same time, there is the fear that greater parliamentary control over appointments might lead to favoritism based on party membership and that judges so chosen could lose their objectivity. The powerful "German Federation of Judges," therefore, is fighting for the right to at least participate in the decision-making process concerning the appointment and promotion of judges. In the civil service the number of politically responsible *Beamte* who are elected by parliamentary assemblies of municipalities, counties, or corporations has increased considerably since 1945. Moreover, legal recognition has been given to a special category of "political *Beamte"* who are required to give loyalty to the main political views and objectives of the government in power. These top ranking *Beamte,* such as state secretaries or leading *Beamte* of the ministries and other responsible offices, can temporarily be furloughed. The majority of *Beamte* do not fall into this category, but they may often feel that their chances of promotion might be better if they are members of a political party. The image of the politically neutral *Beamte* has begun to fade along with the recollection that, after World War II, mere membership in the Nazi party was sufficient cause for discharge. The institution of patronage appears to be growing in Germany, although no empirical research has been undertaken on that topic, probably because nobody is interested in sponsoring such an investigation. There are no figures on how many *Beamte* are members of political parties. Their political influence within the parties can only be measured by their representation in Parliament: The "faction" of *Beamte* is even larger than the "factions" of trade-unionists and attorneys. Such representation (traditional in German Parliaments) constitutes one of the underpinnings of the present system and guarantees that all legislative proposals dealing with *Beamte* will be accorded a favorable hearing.

Prohibition of the strike for the *Beamte*

Today the special status of the *Beamte* is being challenged by a very sharp debate, mostly along ideological lines, as to whether or not all *Beamte* are prohibited from striking.[12] In two states (Bavaria and Rhineland-Palatine) *Beamte* are strictly prohibited from striking, while all other applicable state statutes are silent on this point. Bonn Basic Law, as well as the Weimar Constitution, merely guarantees the right to organize but not the right to strike. Even the traditional term, "freedom to organize" has been replaced by "freedom of association," in order to avoid the misinterpretation of the term as an indirect guarantee of the right to strike. All state constitutions after 1945 have made this distinction between the right to organize and the right to strike. The problem, however, has remained. All *Beamte*, even policemen and soldiers, enjoy complete freedom to organize. But, according to the traditional and prevailing opinion, their organizations are solely lobbying bodies that can only participate in legislative hearings, and the right to be heard is only statutorily guaranteed to "top organization." The natural connection between strike and negotiations does not exist for the *Beamte* organizations and they are not even recognized as being partners in the bargaining process because the laws governing *Beamte* were not the result of collectively negotiated agreements.

Because the laws are generally silent concerning the *Beamte's* access to the strike weapon, the prohibition of all *Beamte* strikes must be seen as flowing from the specific status of *Beamte*, from the obligation of fidelity, or from a fundamental principle underlying the institution of the *Beamtentum*. During the Weimar Republic, this opinion was backed by a nearly unanimous decision of the Reich Parliament to uphold the strike prohibition, after the failure of a large-scale strike of the railway *Beamte* in 1923. Currently, however, the question is under review again. The matter has been reopened because of the confusion arising out of the German Parliament's ratification of the European Social Charter.[13] Article 6 of the Charter gives all employees the right to strike and, according to the language of that document, this would include *Beamte*. The German government, however, interpreted the European Social Charter according to German legal terminology and deposited its interpretation with the General Secretary of the Council of Europe. The German Parliament ratified the European Social Charter, having been assured that no changes in German law would be necessary, and evidently not aware of the steps the government had taken. The question thus arises: What exactly did Parliament ratify, the literal text of the Charter, or the interpretation made by the German government? Is the recognition of the right to strike self-executing? Has Parliament reinterpreted present law by ratifying the Charter, or is that ratification meaningless because it violates Bonn Basic Law? It is clear that lawyers can argue both ways, although at present German lawyers generally tend to ignore the European Social Charter.

Probably, the prohibition of the strike weapon to *Beamte* will be eliminated in the future. Lifetime employment is no longer a bar to strikes, since the argument no longer holds that striking *Beamte* would enjoy the unique privilege of participating in a work stoppage without the usual risk of losing their jobs. In contrast to laws prevailing before 1933, today German labour law does not hold that participation in a strike is reason enough to concede the employer the right to dismiss his employees. German trade unions, both in the private and public sector, often approach a strike gradually by "work to rule," and *Beamte* associations have also followed that practice. During recent years, postal and railroad employees as well as air traffic controllers and tax-officers have followed that practice, and the tactic was tolerated or at least endured by the government. In November 1972, the Union for Education and Science (*Erziehung und Wissenschaft*), a member of the German Confederation of Trade Unions, prepared a ballot on a one-day warning strike of

Hessian teachers. The matter never came to a vote because the Hessian Minister of Education agreed to negotiate with the union. German university professors retaliated against some rather forceful student protests by collectively terminating their courses for a limited time. Others attempted to compel the appointment of a communist applicant. The former action was tacitly approved by the Minister. It remains to be seen whether the latter move will result in disciplinary action. The legal recognition of the right to strike may develop out of this gray zone. It will depend to a great extent on whether or not the *Beamte* themselves are willing to use the strike as a weapon to improve their social position even at the risk of losing former privileges and status. At present, the majority of *Beamte,* especially the older ones, probably would prefer not to take such a drastic step.[14] But in the future they may feel differently. Such a shift in posture would, of course, depend upon employment conditions in the public sector as a whole and the *Beamte* associations' reaction to those conditions.

The organization of the *Beamte* and other employees in the public sector

Public employee unionism in Germany is changing from the older type of organization based on the professional status of the particular employees to associations embracing all workers in a specific branch of public service such as education, health, or public utilities.

Beamte are highly organized compared to the blue-collar and white-collar workers in the public sector.[15] The numbers of *Beamte* claimed by various associations represent 94 percent of the total, but since some *Beamte* are members of more than one association, the actual membership rate may be somewhat less than this figure. The *Beamte* organizations are mainly professional (*berufsstaendische*) associations. Some of them are independent, although the large majority are affiliated with larger confederations.

The most important independent *Beamte* organizations are:

the German Armed Forces Association (*Deutscher bundeswehr-Verband*) with more than 130,000 (80 percent) of the country's professional soldiers;[16] the Union of German Judges (*Deutscher Richterbund*) with about 12,000 judges and state attorneys (the actual title of the association—Union of Judges and State Attorneys in Germany—more closely reflects its composition than does the title ordinarily used), and the University Association (*Hochschulverband*) with 8,000 university professors. The German Federation of Judges is the most influential of the three because of the powerful political role judges have traditionally played.[17]

Most of the rest of the *Beamte* organizations are members of two larger associations: the German Federation of *Beamte* (*Deutscher Beamtenbund*, sometimes translated as the German Civil Servants Association and usually simply referred to as the DBB) and the German *Beamten* Cartel, the top organization of all professional *Beamten* organizations. The DBB,[18] with more than 700,000 members, has both state and federal associations, as does the German *Beamte* Cartel. The latter organization has only about 150,000 members altogether. Additional public sector organizations that are grouped together according to type of work include the Police Trade Union (*Deutsche Polizeigewerkschaft*), the German Post Office Trade Union (*Deutsche Postgewerkschaft*), the Trade Union of Railway Employees of Germany (*Gewerkschaft der Eisenbahner Deutschlands*) and the Education and Science Trade Union. These organizations include all levels of employees whether *Beamte*, white-collar workers, or manual workers, although the *Beamte* are in the majority in each case.

Three of the above-mentioned unions, the postal workers, railway employees, and the Education and Science Trade Union are affiliated with the German Confederation of Trade Unions (DGB), an organization whose member associations, unlike those belonging to the DBB and the Cartel, are drawn from both the public and private sectors. The Police Trade Union, which represents about 75 percent of all organized police officers, is not affiliated with any confederation. It has sought entry into the DGB but thus far has been unsuccessful since that confederation already has an affiliate—the Union for Public Service,

Transport, and Communication (*Gewerkschaft Oeffentliche Dienste, Transport und Verkehr*) that includes some police among its membership and has blocked the entry of the independent organizations as a separate entity within the DGB.

It should be noted that about 10 percent of the DBB's members, despite the organization's title are white-collar *Arbeitnehmer* and, therefore, the DBB includes an "alliance of negotiating unions" capable of making collective agreements, as well as the *Beamte* associations, which are not so empowered. On the other hand, other trade unions have *Beamte,* usually a small minority, among their members. Some associations consider professional status *per se* more important than the distinction between *Beamte* and other employees. This is the case with medical doctors. The Marburg Doctors' Union (*Marburger Bund Angestellter Aerzte*), for example, contains *Beamte* as well as white-collar workers. While this association has some elements that resemble a trade union, there are other professional groups such as the German Lawyers Association or the Central Association of Professional Engineers that merely seek to promote the general interests of their members. It is possible that some of these latter organizations will develop into unions or merge with existing ones.

The Union of Public Service, Transportation, and Communication[19] mentioned earlier includes *Beamte* and other public sector employees and private sector workers as well. It does so because, as indicated earlier, public utilities are sometimes privately owned. On the other hand, the German Union of Salaried Employees (*Deutsche Angestelltengewerkschaft*) has members among white-collar workers from the public as well as the private sector, and even includes some *Beamte,* largely those who were promoted from among white-collar workers.

As the above description indicates, membership in public employee associations is no longer based solely upon status. Yet, even when the organization embraces all workers in a particular branch of government, its substructure always has separate sections for *Beamte* and *Arbeitnehmer,* since the two groups are treated differently under the law. However, because the *Arbeit-*

nehmer in those organizations can negotiate collective agreements, they are in a position, even if indirectly, to influence the salary scales set for their *Beamte* brethren. The wage increases they receive through negotiation generally serve as a yardstick to determine the salaries the *Beamte* will receive.

Theoretically, there is some dispute as to whether or not white-collar *Arbeitnehmer* in the public sector have the right to strike. In practice, government negotiators always recognize the possibility that a strike could, in fact, occur.

Collective bargaining is carried on at three levels of government: federal, state, and local. Ordinarily, individual states do not negotiate alone. Instead, they have banded together into the Bargaining Association of German States (*Tarifgemeinschaft der Deutschen Laender*), and that organization acts for them. The same holds for negotiations at the local level, with the Federation of Local Government Employers Association (*Vereinigung der Kommunalen Arbeitgeberverbaender*) as the bargaining agent.

The policy at all levels of government is to negotiate first with the most powerful organization they must deal with. They then negotiate similar or identical collective agreements with the rest. German labour law does not oblige employers to bargain with all of the associations to which their employees may belong. Thus, the employers also are free to give preference to the trade unions with the widest jurisdiction among their membership because then they can set salary rates for employees of the greatest number of different occupations. In the winter of 1972-73, this policy caused the federal government a certain amount of discomfort because the pilots' association was dissatisfied with the results of the negotiations carried out on their behalf by the Union of Public Service, Transportation, and Communication. Initially, the pilots demanded to be recognized as a separate bargaining unit and threatened to strike to enforce that demand. However, in the end the matter was settled peaceably.

The problem of collective bargaining immediately leads to the decisive question of social status, i.e., how does the social status of *Beamte* compare with that of other employees?

The process of social equalization

A comparison between the situation of *Arbeitnehmer* and of *Beamte* in the year 1873, when the first *Reichbeamte* Act was promulgated, and the situation today clearly shows to what extent the two groups have moved towards one another in the last 100 years. In 1873, the old, sick, or unemployed *Arbeitnehmer* depended entirely on the voluntary beneficence of his former employer, his religious community, his trade-union, or his municipality. He worked under the permanent threat of losing his job since his employer could dismiss him at any time. In contrast, the *Beamte* was socially protected throughout his lifetime and could not be dismissed. The state had to take care of him (the so-called principle of alimentation) in case of sickness or disability. He received a pension and his wife and children were supported after his death.

These basic distinctions were diminished when social insurance was introduced in 1883, 1884, 1889 and finally in 1927 (legislation providing for unemployment compensation). Since that legislation was enacted, even manual workers have received paid sick leave. Since 1920, the statutes have protected workers against arbitrary dismissal and such cases are subject to review by works councils and labour courts. Guaranteed full employment, a basic difference between *Beamte* and *Arbeitnehmer* has also disappeared. Since the "economic miracle" following the nearly total destruction of the German economy by the Second World War, Germany has achieved full employment and, considering the two and a half million foreign workers, even over employment. Mass unemployment is something that only people over 60 years old and a handful of historians remember. Thus, the *Beamte's* privileged "social security" has become less important than before.

The working conditions of the *Beamte* and those of white-collar workers (who often hold comparable positions) have become more and more alike.[20] *Beamte* were the first to receive paid holidays, but the *Arbeitnehmer*, by means of collective agreements, court decisions, and constitutions and statutes, followed. As to shorter work weeks, the *Arbeitnehmer* led the way, first with the demand for a 48-hour week (followed by further diminutions), and the *Beamte* followed. The same holds true with regard to the lengthening of vacation periods and the institution of the principle of co-determination.[21] The Works Constitution Act restricted management decisions regarding personnel questions and the Staff Representation Act reluctantly went along in order to forestall the prospect of poorer performance on the job.

In the public sector, the institution of the principle of co-determination is not, as in private industry, held in check by the possibility of bankruptcy. But the council system is still counterbalanced by the principle of responsibility to democratically elected bodies. In one area, however, the council system has won out. In the German universities "progressive" statutes have given students, teaching assistants, nontenured faculty, and nonacademic employees a majority voice in the decision-making process.

The gap between salaries paid to *Beamte* and *Arbeitnehmer*, once considerable, has narrowed appreciably and the *Beamte* have come to feel that they are the disadvantaged, since they have not benefitted from the process of liberalizing labour conditions to the extent that the *Arbeitnehmer* have. This feeling is widespread and explains why the *Beamte's* attitude towards strike action has recently changed from one of complete condemnation to a less decided position, or even a reluctant acceptance of the idea. The *Beamte* are aware that the threat of strikes has improved the social position of the *Arbeitnehmer* and that it could be an effective instrument for them to use to regain their former superior status *vis-à-vis* the *Arbeitnehmer*.[22] This process of equalization has flowed both ways. Certainly the door has been opened for new conditions as to working time or length of vacations, and the like. *Beamte* are now demanding overtime pay and a thirteenth month's salary, which the other public sector white-collar workers already receive. On the other hand, principles of the *Beamtentum* such as the duty to obey, the oath to follow the basic law and the statutes, the regulations concerning promotion, and the prohibition of dismissal except for just cause now apply to the white-collar workers as well. Some distinctions with regard to disciplinary sanctions, rules governing the transfer to other jobs, and certain sick pay benefits are still reserved for the *Beamte*. Generally, however, equalization prevails. This is especially true of responsibility for criminal acts. The provisions governing *Beamte* in the Penal Code place them under the same liabilities as white-collar *Arbeitnehmer* exercising the same functions. State liability for damages caused by *Beamte* has also now been extended to white-collar workers holding comparable offices.

These observations set the stage for a prognosis on future German legal development.

Future German legal development

The suggestions that follow on how to improve the *Beamtentum* institution would, if taken, not lead to major changes but rather to minor ones that would result in greater efficiency within public administration. The Confederation of German Trade Unions has proposed the adoption of the Swedish model under which the regulations governing *Beamte* wages, hours, and working conditions would be basically set by statute, but with some subject areas determined by the collective bargaining process. Despite the fact that a legal argument could be made that such a system would be constitutional in Germany, the Confederation proposal will not be acted upon favorably.[23]

It may well be that the amorphous grouping of the *Beamtentum* will be divided more and more into groups of employees performing the same functions. A beginning has been made with the promulgation of special statutes for judges (German Judge Act of 1961/72), for police officers (1960/67), for professional soldiers (1969), and for the universities. It may be the case that all public employees in the security branch, as well as *Beamte* in confidential posts and those with managerial functions, will maintain their current special status. If so, the legal distinction drawn between these *Beamte* and the rest could reinstitute the feudal concept of separation of state and society. It is questionable that guaranteed lifetime employment will be abolished for the other *Beamte,* even if full employment comes to be recognized as a government obligation. This development could occur, however, if public sector employees increased their desire to change jobs several times during their working lives. One problem must be solved: Public utilities cannot continue to be legally treated differently depending upon the public or private identity of the employer.[24] A common set of regulations must be developed.

It is very likely that legislation will be enacted that will guarantee an employee's right to his job in the private sector. Industry in Germany is undergoing a process of economic concentration that can be slowed, but not halted, by antitrust legislation. The fear of mass unemployment stemming from the experiences of 1933 may lead to a governmental determination to subsidize or take over bankrupt companies, as it did in the case of Krupp several years ago, so that the workers in those industries can retain their jobs. This would extend the principle of guaranteed employment from the public to the private sector. Another characteristic of the public sector—an ever increasing bureaucracy—may also be reflected in the private sector. Increase in company size and the extension of the principle of co-determination would be equally responsible for the development of that phenomenon in the private sector. Such changes, however, will not happen overnight; instead, the process will be a gradual one.

Appendix A

Union Membership Rates, 12/31/71
(in thousands)

	Total Employment	*Total Union Membership*	*Percent Union Membership*
Manual workers	12,524	5,089	40%
White-collar workers	7,832	1,507	19%
Beamte	1,451	1,372	94%

Appendix B
Public Service (1971)

Employer	Beamte (%)	White-collar workers (%)	Manual workers (%)	Total Employment
Federal Republic	80,817 (27.9)	100,389 (34.5)	108,997 (37.6)	290,203
Town states*	100,457 (42.4)	98,848 (41.9)	36,660 (15.7)	235,965
Other states	626,182 (64.1)	281,296 (28.8)	69,875 (7.1)	977,353
Municipalities (and their associations)	138,033 (19.8)	352,114 (50.6)	206,126 (29.6)	696,273
Economic enterprises	10,722 (7.4)	37,028 (24.8)	101,436 (67.8)	149,186
Regional corporations	956,211 (40.7)	869,675 (37.0)	523,094 (22.3)	2,348,980
German federal railway	221,407 (52.4)	9,889 (2.4)	190,505 (45.2)	421,801
German federal post	258,255 (60.4)	57,780 (13.6)	111,109 (26.0)	427,144
TOTAL	1,435,873 (44.9)	937,344 (29.3)	824,708 (25.8)	3,197,925

* Berlin, Hamburg, and Bremen.

Source: *Wirtschaft und Statistik* 1972, p. 282.

1. Books on labour law, therefore, do not deal with *Beamte* (with one exception, cf. footnote 24). *Beamte* are the subject of special monographs: Alfred Bochalli, *Grundriss des deutschen Beamtenrechts;* Botho Bauch, *Das Recht der Beamten* 1966 where their legal status is described as part of special administrative law (cf. footnote 2) or as part of the public service (cf. footnote 4).

2. Public law includes administrative law, which includes law for *Beamte.* Therefore, the monographs of administrative law (e.g. Hans J. Wolff, *Verwaltungsrecht* vol. 2 1970 or Ingo von Muench (ed.), *Besonderes Verwaltungsrecht* 1970) are useful.

3. The disciplinary courts controlling minor disciplinary sanctions and deciding on the major ones (forced retirement and discharge or diminution of salary or transfer to another office) are either established as special courts or as parts of administrative courts. With their tripartite structure they resemble the labour courts.

4. Cf. Carl Hermann Ule, *Oeffentlicher Dienst* in Bettermann and Nipperdey (ed.), *Die Grundrechte* vol. IV, 2, 1962, p. 357 and William H. McPherson, *Public Employee Relations in West Germany,* Ann Arbor: Institute of Labor and Industrial Relations, 1971.

5. Cf. Appendix B.

6. Cf. Joerg Jung, *Die Zweispurigkeit des Oeffentlichen Dienstes. Eine Untersuchung über die Veraenderung der Personalstruktur im oeffentlichen Dienst und die Verankerung des Berufsbeamtentums im Grundgesetz,* Duncker und Humbolt Verlag Berlin 1971, p. 49.

7. The German word is *"Vereinigung,"* which has not been defined by Bonn Basic Law. But article 9, section 1 speaks of the right of all Germans to form associations and companies *(Vereine und Gesellschafter)*—both terms may be used and are used to define the word *"Vereinigung."* This interpretation is satisfactory as long as the constitutional guarantee is understood to include all forms of alliances, temporary or permanent. The dispute over interpretation is important in practice because it involves the question of whether article 9, section 3 Bonn Basic Law indirectly gives nonunion members the right to strike. Cf. Thilo Ramm, *Der nichtgewerkschaftliche Streik,* in *Arbeit und Recht* vol. 19 (1971) p. 87.

8. Cf. Lotz, *Geschichte des deutschen Beamtentums* 1909 and Isaacson, *Geschichte des preussischen Beamtentums,* 3 Vol. 1878 and 1883.

9. Cf. Michael Kirn, *Verfassungsumsturz oder Rechtskontinuitaet. Die Stellung der Jurisprudenz nach 1945 zum Dritten Reich, insbesondere die Konflikte um die Kontinuitaet der Beamtenrechte und Art 131,* Grundgesetz, 1972.

10. Terminology again reflect ideological roots: The *general* relationship of subordination existed between the monarch and the subject. Both terms are still used by German public lawyers, cf. Wilhelm Paetzold, *Die Abgrenzung vom allgemeinen und besonderen Gewaltverhaeltnis.* Dissertation Hamburg Law Faculty 1972.

11. Cf. *Wortlaut under Kritik der verfassungswidrigen Januarbeschluesse. Materialien fuer Studenten, Beamte, Angestellte und Arbeiter im oeffentlichen Dienst* 1972 Pahl-Rugenstein-Verlag Cologne. This pamphlet also includes all of the arguments made against these resolutions, but none made in favor of their legality.

12. Cf. Wolfgang Daeubler, *Der Streik im oeffentlichen Dienst* 1970, 1971.

Mohr-Verlag, Tuebingen, Thilo Ramm, *Das Koalition-under Streikrecht der Beamten.* Bund-Verlag, Cologne 1970, Josef Isense, *Beamtenstreik, Zur rechtlichen Zulaessigkeit des Dienstkampfes* 1971, Goldesberger Taschenbuch-Verlag GmbH, ferner Friedrich E. Schnapp, *Beamtenstreik-Eine Zwischenbilanz, Die oeffentliche Verwaltung* 1973, p. 32.

13. Cf. for the following the conclusions of the committee of independent experts on the European Social Charter (Council of Europe), Vol. I, 1970, p. 185 and Vol. II, 1971, p. 28 and the second report of the governmental committee adopted on 8 September 1972, p. 14. The German Federal Government has been asked by the Federal Government Committee to review the situation.

14. Cf. Franz Ronneberger und Udo Roedel, *Beamte im gesellschaftlichen Wandlungsprozess. Soziale Stellung und soziales Bewusstsein von Beamten in der Bundesrepublik,* Godesberger Taschenbuch-Verlag, 1971.

15. Cf. Appendix A.

16. Cf. Hermann Giesen, *Der Deutsche Bundeswehr-Verband,* Bonn, 1970.

17. Teachers are organized in different associations, but it may well be that the "Teacher Association" established in 1969 will emerge as the dominant one.

18. Cf. *Deutscher Beamtenbund Ursprung, Weg, Ziel-Bad-Godesberg Deutscher Beamtenverlag,* 1968.

19. Cf. Furtwängler, ÖTV. *Die Geschichte einer Gewerkschaft,* Stuttgart-Union—Druckerei, 1955, 2. Aufl. und ÖTV, 20 Jahre ÖTV, Stuttgart-Verlagsanstalt Courier 1966.

20. Cf. Winfried Benz, *Beamtenverhaeltnis und Arbeitsverhaeltnis,* Stuttgart, 1969; Gustav Fischer Verlag and Manfred Loewisch, *Beamtenrecht—eigen staendiges Recht oder Teil des Arbeitsrechts,* in Genscher and others, *Der oeffentliche Dienst am Scheidweg,* 1972, Godesberger Taschenbuch Verlag.

21. The draft of a new federal Personal Staff Act, which should replace the act of 1955 and was modelled after the Works Constitution Act of 1972, was submitted to the German Federal Parliament in August 1972, but did not pass because of the dissolution of the parliament. Now the draft will be introduced again. Cf. on the general problem of co-determination in the public service Walter Leisner, *Mitbestimmung im oeffentlichen Dienst,* 1970, Godesberger Taschenbuch Verlag.

22. Cf. Ferdinand Matthey, *Zur Rechtsangleichung bei Beamten und Angestellten im oeffentlichen Dienst* 1971 Fundament Verlag Dr. Sasse, Hamburg; and Walter Wiese, *Der Staatsdienst in der Bundesrepublik Deutschland.* Grundlagen, Probleme, Neuordnung, 1972, Luchterhand Verlag Neuwied.

23. This prediction has now been confirmed as reflected in the reform proposals concerning public service legislation made by the majority of a commission of experts called together by the Federal Minister of Interior at the request of the Federal Parliament ("*Bericht der Studienkommission fuer die Reform des oeffentlichen Dienstrechts,*" 1973 Nomos Verlagsgesellschaft Baden-Baden").

24. Cf. as a survey of the present situation Guenter Puettner, *Die Oeffentlichen Unternehman. Verfassungsfragen zur wirtschaftlichen betaetigung der oeffentlichen Hand,* 1969, Gehlen Verlag, Homburg.

7

Labour Relations in the Public Sector in Austria

*Theodor Tomandl**

I N discussing problems of labour relations in the public sector, we should confirm at the beginning that there has been almost no research program in Austria up to now. Hence, the statements and opinions expressed in this chapter more or less reflect the personal views of the author. The Austrian Association for Industrial Relations, however, has already decided to deal with this subject in greater depth in the future.

Labour relations in the public sector cannot be analyzed in an isolated way. There are four main issues to be discussed: the organization of the state and its machinery, the legal conception of the contrast between private and public law, the impact of state activities on the private sector of the economy, and, last but not least, the general goals and framework of industrial relations.

Organization of the Austrian republic

Austria is a federal republic of nine states that each have a legislature and an executive. Each state is subdivided into municipal-

*Director, Institute of Labour Law and Law of Social Security, University of Vienna.

ities entitled to run selected affairs in self-government. Austria is a democracy in the Western sense of the word and, in legal terms, is a constitutional state ·governed by statute law rather than by common law. The Austrian Constitution has defined the respective powers of the Republic and the states. Legislation on and administration of the most important matters rest with the Republic but, as a rule, the Republic has done without agencies of its own for direct administration. Federal administration is most frequently done by state agencies under the aegis of the federal minister concerned. On the other hand, unless the right is reserved for the Republic, the states are entitled to pass legislation on any matter and to administer their own affairs. Consequently, there is no uniform legislation regarding the public service. In principle, the Republic's labour relations legislation is restricted to federal employees. The labour relations of state and municipal employees are governed by state law. This paper will focus on federal labour relations.

Private law versus public law

The separation of private law and public law is the foundation of the Austrian legal system. Public law deals with the hierarchy of the state, e.g., the procedure adopted by state authorities, the status of citizens, and the relations between officials and individuals. Its main parts are constitutional law and administrative law. On the other hand, private law is said to be the law of men communicating on equal terms, the law governing the mutual relationships of free men. More and more, however, it has become obvious that this strict separation stressed by legal doctrine cannot be rigidly upheld in practice. Nevertheless, the fundamental consequence of this separation means that a completely different system of legal protection exists for civil cases from the system that covers cases of public law.

Under civil law, individuals are at liberty to regulate their own affairs according to their free will. The predominant instrument of regulation is the contract, but this does not mean that there is unlimited freedom. Limitations are imposed on free men in order to safeguard the vital interests of individuals and the community. In case of a dispute, each individual is entitled to apply to the courts.

On the other hand, under public law there is the obligation of every official to execute the law and to refrain from discretionary measures. According to the principle of separation of powers, the administration is strictly bound by the law. In the sector of public law, however, there are no courts to deal with complaints, only administrative bodies acting under the control of the federal or national government. Under certain conditions, the Administrative Court may over rule decisions of the highest administrative authorities. Whereas a judge is guaranteed independence, officials who are members of administrative bodies are subject to the directives of their superior authorities and may be removed in case of opposition. Finally, in public law, the fundamental rights of man have to be respected in a direct way. Fundamental rights may be defended by everyone before the Constitutional Court. On the contrary, in civil law fundamental rights are effective in an indirect way at most.

Legislation, as a rule, has virtual discretionary power to shape certain legal relations either in terms of public law or in terms of civil law.

The state as a subject of civil law

The above-mentioned limitations of public law (liability to statutes, terms of reference, parliamentary control, and fundamental rights) have frequently stimulated a movement of the state toward civil law. The Republic, the states, and municipalities have acted as individuals; have done so without decrees, edicts, and orders; have entered into contracts; and have acted as entrepreneurs. In this way the state has extended its range of competence. Disregarding the constitutional limitations imposed on them, the Republic and the states act as "individuals" as they see fit. They run enterprises, grant subsidies, place orders, and so on. As a result, the Austrian economy is highly infiltrated by state-owned enterprises, and it is estimated that about three-quarters of the stocks available in Austria are held by the state. The main part of basic industry and the banking system are state-owned. Many companies are state-owned while others are controlled to a considerable extent by the state. In the sector of public utilities, the Republic, the states, and the municipalities usually carry on these functions as part of their governmental activities.

Industrial relations

Industrial relations in Austria are in general characterized by the neutrality of the state. Parliament has provided a comprehensive labour law that regulates basic terms of employment, the legal effects of collective agreements, and the institution of workers' councils on the factory level. However, wage policy and the improvement of other labour conditions are under the joint control of the trade unions and the employers' organizations. Austria has a freely-elected and independent comprehensive trade union movement. The *Österreichischer Gewerkschaftsbund* (ÖGB—Austrian Trade Union Confederation) is supposedly the most powerful organization in Austria. On the other hand, there are strong central organizations of industrial and agricultural employers.

Austria is famous for its industrial peace, a consequence of the spirit of social partnership that has been built by the trade unions and the employers' organizations since 1945. The basic instrument of social progress is the collective agreement. Each party covered by the collective agreement has the right to enforce its terms. Strikes seem to be rather outdated in modern Austria; industrial conflicts are settled by negotiations. During the negotiations the president of the ÖGB, the presidents of the employers' organizations, and, last but not least, the Cabinet frequently act as mediators. As a result, the ÖGB, has developed a strong feeling of responsibility at the same time that it has expanded its influence on Austrian economic policy.

Patterns of employment in the public service

Public employees fall into three different categories.

Regular employees

In state-owned companies employees are governed by the common labour law that covers employees in privately-owned enterprises. Moreover, these companies are members of employers' organizations and are bound by the general collective agreement of their industry or trade. In addition, there are workers' councils in these enterprises. In fact, employees in state-owned companies differ from those in privately-owned enterprises in only one respect: political influences are more visible in the management and in the workers' councils of the state-owned companies. To become a member of the board of directors or of the supervisory board of state-owned companies, a candidate needs a good deal of patronage by political parties. On the worker side a party faction usually backs a candidate in the election of the workers' council in the state-owned companies. An informal coalition is sometimes formed between managers and members of the workers' council belonging to the same political party. Thus, as far as labour relations are concerned there is no difference between state-owned and privately-owned enterprises; however, for reasons we shall see below, Austrians object to the idea that these jobs are to be regarded as part of the public sector.

Public employees

Employees engaged in government administration, public utilities, public services and agencies are not affected by common labour law. There are two alernatives to be considered. These alternatives are equally applicable to professional employees, white-collar workers, and manual workers.

(i) Public employees may be covered by civil contracts, in which case they are called *Vertragsbedienstete*. The terms of their contracts are governed by special labour law. There is an extensive federal statute regulating their labour relations (*Vertragsbedienstetengesetz* 1948, *Bundesgesetzblatt*—BGBI. Nr. 86/1948), and there are similar national statutes for the *Vertragsbedienstete* of the states. In the case of a dispute, these civil servants are entitled to start proceedings in the labour courts. Their duties and rights are similar to those of employees in private firms, except that their salaries and working conditions are directly fixed by statutes. These statutes are ordinarily the result of conferences and agreement between the Joint Commission for Prices and Wages and the Joint Bargaining Board. However, in exceptional cases, the terms of employment may be negotiated, but these special contracts must be approved by the Federal Chancellor and the Minister of Finance. *Vertragsbedienstete* are guaranteed job protection and can only be fired on certain grounds such as negligence. This group of public employees also receives the normal social security benefits. In the course of this chapter I shall call these *Vertragsbedienstete,* or *contract employees.*

(ii) Public employees may also be appointed by the government, in which case there is no contract. Instead, the employer unilaterally formulates the labour conditions. The applicant can then either accept or reject the appointment. In practice, however, the public employer has little discretionary power in shaping the terms of employment. Wages, working hours, duties, and rights have been fixed by statute (see *Dienstpragmatik Reichsgesetzblatt* Nr. 15/1914 and the *Gehaltsgesetz Bundesgesetzblatt* Nr. 54/1956). Nor are the hiring agencies permitted to improve the personal rights of an employee unless there is a special statute available. In other words, the hiring of this type of public employee *(Beamte)* is covered by public law and is rigidly fixed by statute. A complaint, therefore, cannot be brought to court but must be handled by a superior authority. An individual labour dispute has to be settled according to the ponderous rules of administrative procedure. *Beamte* are appointed for life and, unless they commit a gross error or become incapable of work, they cannot be fired. However, they have to retire at age 65.

Salaries are paid according to a complex scheme (see *Gehaltsgesetz* 1956, BGBI. Nr. 54/1956), which is based on a wage increase every two years accompanied by a special increase on the occasion of a promotion. Promotion, however, is dependent upon seniority. These public employees are partly covered by the general social security program (health insurance, workmen's compensation), and partly by their own schedule, which offers a better old-age pension plan. From here on, *Beamte* will be called civil servants.

In the past, the use of civil servants was an adequate means for pursuing administrative affairs and giving the government a helping hand. Contract employees were originally appointed to public-owned agencies or employed for various kinds of nongovernmental tasks. It was not until the end of the 19th century that this conception changed. Nowadays there is no legal obstacle to engaging a contract employee to do governmental work or to employing a civil servant to deal with nongovernmental affairs. In other words, the two have become completely interchangeable. Many important jobs in a ministry are held by contract employees. Despite this fact, civil servants are, according to the prevailing philosophy and the interpretation by those concerned, quite different from contract employees. They consider themselves to be a privileged class, although on the same type of job there is no perceptible difference between the duties of a civil servant and a contract employee. However, most of the superior positions in a ministry are entrusted to civil servants.

A final reference to terminology: civil servants and contract employees will be jointly referred to as public employees in this chapter.

Austrian labour statistics do not include data on the number of public employees. Although the government is obliged to produce annual reviews of the number of federal employees, these reviews do not show the actual number of persons employed.[1] It is estimated that the total number of public employees in the service of the Republic, the states, and municipalities may be about 450,000, a third of them being contract employees. The number of employees working in state-owned enterprises is unknown.

Interdependence of private sector labour law and public service law

Labour conditions

An undeniable interdependence exists between the development of private sector labour law and special law concerning civil servants and contract employees. It is not easy, however, to find out which has taken the lead. During the 19th century the public sector was clearly ahead. In its present-day meaning, labour law did not exist and the status of public employees, especially that of the civil servants, who already guaranteed by statute. Therefore, employees in the private sector tried to achieve a similar position. At the forefront were the white-collar workers, notably the clerks. Hence, the sequence of labour standards in those days was: public employees, clerks, industrial workers.

After World War I things changed. Starting in 1919, workers' councils had to be elected in all enterprises employing more than 20 employees and collective agreements were also negotiated to guarantee minimum labour standards for all industries and trades. Moreover, individual labour law was shaped by numerous statutes. The unique position of public employees vanished as industrial workers and salaried employees in the private sector took the lead in fighting for and achieving improved labour conditions. At the present time, there is practically no substantial disparity between the wages and working conditions of contract employees and civil servants in the same kinds of jobs. However, civil servants still have three advantages over contract employees: better chances for promotion, a special old-age benefit scheme, and more job security.

Since 1945 public employees have been represented within the Austrian Trade Union Confederation (ÖGB) by four of the existing 16 unions: the railway workers, postal wage earners, municipal employees, and employees of the Republic and the states. In organizational matters there is no difference between contract employees and civil servants. The membership rate within these unions seems to be very high. It is estimated that about 95 percent of the railwaymen, 90 percent of the postal workers, and 60-67 percent of the employees of the Republic and the states are organized. The average membership rate of workers in unions and belonging to the Austrian Trade Union Confederation is said to exceed 66 percent.

These four unions have formed a Joint Bargaining Board to negotiate with the state-employer. This must not be understood as a contradiction to the earlier statement that labour conditions of public employees are directly governed by statutes. One must distinguish between the form and the substance, however. It is true that in a formal sense these statutes have been issued unilaterally by Parliament. As to the content of the statutes, however, frequently a bargain has been struck between the Joint Bargaining Board, on the one hand, and the government represented by the Federal Chancellor and the Minister of Finance on the other hand. Although the outcome of these negotiations does not formally bind Parliament, Parliament has never been non-compliant once a compromise in this bargaining process has been achieved. However, when the bargaining parties fail to reach an informal agreement beforehand, one cannot predict what the government will do. Sometimes it will insist on its previously held position, sometimes not.

The Joint Bargaining Board negotiates with the Austrian Government, which is represented by the Federal Chancellor and the Federal Minister of Finance. The Federal Chancellor is responsible for carrying out the federal law of public service and the Minister of Finance is responsible for its financing. On the other hand, the Federal Minister of Social Affairs, who is normally the leading man in industrial relations, plays almost no role with public employees. As a Cabinet member, he is entitled to participate in decision making, as are the other members of this body.

Therefore, over the past decades the public sector has not made any significant contribution to the general development of new standards for labour conditions. The results of collective bargaining in the private sector have almost without exception served as a model for subsequent negotiations in the public service and have been most effective in decreasing working hours and increasing paid holidays. As already mentioned, the private sector has not set a precedent for the salary scales of the public sector, although until now the trade unions of the public sector have been influenced by the general wage pattern of the private sector in bargaining for higher wages. A new method has now been adopted in the public sector whereby the government provides for annual wage increases together with an automatic adjustment in the case of a rise in the cost of living. Civil servants have some advantages in job protection and old-age benefits although the trade unions of private employees have gradually achieved approximately the same conditions through lobbying for various amendments to federal statutes. It is quite possible that, ultimately, any substantial difference in old-age benefits will disappear in future adjustments at the factory level. In my opinion, however, life employment will remain a special advantage of civil servants.

Safety and health at work

The conduct of the trade unions of employees in the public sector is somewhat different from that of other unions. Public employees seem to be more traditional, more impressed by authority, and milder in their actions. In other words, they are conservatives. This does not mean that their unions work without success. Although there have been very few strikes in the public sector, there is a scarcity of strikes in Austria in general. However, one result of this conduct should be mentioned. Trade unions of the public sector have not been successful in improving standards of industrial safety and health protection for their members. In the private sector, there are comprehensive statutes and decrees concerning this matter, which are controlled by a specialized administrative body called the factory inspectorate (*Arbeitsinspektorat*). However, the public sector lacks the same means to secure safety and health at work and needs a controlling authority. In fact there are certain branches of the public service where the labour conditions flagrantly violate even the most basic standards of hygiene already established in the private sector. Finance offices and university institutes, for example, frequently lack sufficient air circulation, natural light, and hygienic facilities. The unions have made many demands along these lines and a bill has been in preparation for years, but so far the problem has not been settled. It is unbelievable that a problem of this importance has not already been settled by unions of the public sector.

Participation in decision making

Another problem is the participation of the employees in the process of decision making. In public enterprises, the employees are entitled to elect workers' councils, which act as independent bodies. Responsibility rests entirely with the employees since these workers' councils have been empowered by law (*Betriebsrätegesetz* 1947, BGBl. No. 97/1947) with substantial rights, and the unlimited power formerly exercised by the employer to direct work has been greatly reduced in personal, social, and economic matters. Workers' councils not only have to be informed ahead of time about all plans of the employer concerning the workers' interests but in addition are entitled to object to certain plans and even to hinder certain measures of the employer of which they do not approve. For example, a worker may not be transferred to another job without the consent of the workers' council; if a dispute should arise between the employer and the workers' council over such a question, the employer is entitled to bring his demand before a specialized administrative board, (the *Einigungsamt*), which is authorized to settle the case. The transfer of the worker's position may be effective only if this board is in agreement with the employer. If an employer has dismissed an employee, the workers' council may object and take action to overrule the dismissal. Once again, the above-mentioned administrative board is entitled to declare the dismissal null and void. Some other examples may show the importance of these councils. The determination of daily working hours within the framework of the statutory 42 hour week, work breaks, and methods of calculating wages are no longer subjects that the employer is permitted to regulate unilaterally. In these, and in other questions, he must try to reach an agreement with the workers' council. What is the position of public employees in regard to these questions? Public employees have long demanded similar workers' councils, but it was not until 1967 that Parliament passed a Personnel Representation Act. (*Personalvertretungsgesetz*, BGBl. Nr. 133/1967).

There are, however, two conspicuous differences between workers' councils in private enterprises and personnel representative councils in the public service. First of all, there is a different legal construction under the constitutional law. Personnel representative councils have been modelled on bodies corporate and, according to our constitution, such bodies are not controlled by state organs but have to submit to governmental supervision. Thus, a specialized supervisory board headed by a judge has been created. Second, according to another principle laid down in the Austrian Constitution, a Minister is not bound by the directives or decisions of any other person or body in executing his parliamentary responsibility. It has been argued that substantial participation of personnel representative councils similar to that of the workers' councils in decision making would be an infringement of this principle. It follows that personnel representative councils are restricted to the right to be informed of any planned activity concerning labour conditions and to the right to take part in discussing all employee concerns but have been cut off from any participation in decision making. The final step the personnel representative councils can take is to ask for the opinion of the above-mentioned supervisory board, which the Minister is then at liberty to accept or reject.

These personnel representative councils deal not only with civil servants but also with contract employees. The important distinction is whether or not such an office belongs within the sphere of governmental administration. If so, then a personnel representative council has to be elected; if not (which means the entity in question is a proprietary industry), a workers' council has to be elected.

In spite of the limited power of the personnel representative councils, we should state that 1967 was the starting point of a new period of labour relations in the public sector. Ministers and supervisory officials can no longer ignore the concerns of their staff. An information and feedback process began in 1967, the full consequences of which have not yet been seen. Several results, however, are already visible. Supervisors can no longer behave as sovereigns, and any measure that is likely to affect the interests of employees must be accounted for. The effectiveness of the personnel representative councils nevertheless is to some extent related to party membership. Events have shown that personnel representatives whose sympathies lie with opposition parties have been more active than those following the political beliefs of the Minister in power. It is unlikely that this phenomenon will soon end.

One of the most discussed problems in Austria over the past years has been that of workers' participation in management. The law currently provides for such participation only in corporations. In these companies the workers' councils are entitled to nominate two representatives to become members of the supervisory board. By company law, this supervisory board is empowered to appoint the managing board of the enterprise and to supervise its activity. Certain measures of the managing boards need the approval of the supervisory board. Depending on its by-laws, each company is at liberty to fix the number of supervisory board members at between three and seven. It is therefore to be assumed that the additional two employee members are a minority group. The ruling Socialist Party, however, has prepared a bill providing for strengthening this minority. In the future, employees are to have a one-third representation on the supervisory board. This plan will first take effect with the impending amalgamation of the two most important Austrian steel companies, both of which are completely state owned. After a period of time, the new plan is to be extended to all private and state-owned corporations.

Participation in the management of governmental administration has not yet been discussed. The universities provide the one exception. A new organizational plan for Austrian universities has been drafted by the Minister, providing for participation of students, assistants, and clerks as well as faculty in the governance of the university. Professors will be deprived of their majority and are to be reduced to being a minority group. Students demand that professors, assistants, and students should each have one-third representation. As noted, this is the one case in the public administrative sector where the problems of participation in management have been under discussion.

Basic problems of public employees

Administrative reform

There seem to be two possible causes for most of the problems related to public employees. The first is the fact that the structure and organization of public administration were developed in the 18th and 19th centuries, whereas modern industrial law is a creature of the 20th century. The second cause refers to constitutional change. An institution originally created to safeguard administration in an absolute and, later, a constitutional monarchy, which adhered to a limited concept of governmental duties, is currently confronted with a pluralistic party state in a society that forces those in government to continuously extend their activities. Of course the public service program has been frequently modified and adjusted but the basic pattern is derived from an outmoded period. The present effects of this basic pattern shall be shown in some examples.

Civil servants have been put into an ambiguous position. On the one hand, the modern conception of the state has extended state influence to a degree formerly unknown, especially in the fiield of social and economic policy. As a consequence, not only has the number of public employees steadily increased but a diversification of jobs has also taken place. On the other hand, in spite of the increase in the quantity and quality of activity, public opinion holds public employees in much lower esteem. Widespread prejudice identifies public service with bureaucracy, ineffective work, and outdated management practices, and the demand for a far-reaching administrative reform has had support from all political factions. So far, according to mass media, all attempts of present and former governments to bring forth such a reform have failed. Although no basic reform has been carried out, this does not imply that nothing has been done. Austrian governments have preferred a gradual reform policy and in fact there have been many minor changes. Before the 1960s, there was a monopoly of law school graduates in those jobs requiring academic training. In the last decade, however, more and more social science graduates have succeeded in being employed in public service jobs. This new staff, combined with the installation of computers, is supposed to change the traditional patterns of management from the foundations up. In addition, the government has announced its intention of improving training. A specialized Administration Academy is to be founded to provide post-graduate training for public employees. Recently a Secretary of State for labour relations has been appointed in the public service. The government, in other words, has emphasized evolution instead of sudden reform.

Practice has shown that plans to reform the public service cannot succeed unless the trade unions and the rank and file support these ideas. This support has been formally and repeatedly offered in public but, in fact, the unions seem to defend their own interests and traditions like watch-dogs. It may be that in preparing for administrative reform, the government has failed to sufficiently educate and enlighten those concerned with its goals about their part in this process and their status when the new plan is established. Public opinion, moreover, tends to regard the government as not acting seriously enough in putting through its reforms, and suspects public employees of practising obstruction.

Impact of party politics

Public employees should have become an important pressure group. Political leaders cannot do without the advice and information of higher officials and, as a result, public employees as well as functionaries of other pressure groups dominate more and more in Parliament and the Cabinet. There is a reason for this development. Politicians who are engaged as public employees are granted sufficient time off to carry out political functions, whereas self-employed men never have time to spare. However, once a public employee becomes a politician, a peculiar kind of change takes place sooner or later. Usually he ceases to act as a representative of the pressure group of public employees, which is a direct consequence of the lack of prestige of public employees. A politician fears being regarded as representing the interests of public employees. And this may be another reason why the trade unions of public employees sometimes fail to carry out their point.

Another urgent question refers to the influence of party politics. There has been a tendency in all governments to engage or promote political friends rather than opponents. The results of this attitude are related to the pattern of government. During the period of coalition in the government the two big Austrian parties tried to effect a balance. In "black" ministries, partisans of the People's Party could more realistically expect to be hired and promoted by its parties' ministers than those adhering to the "red" Socialist Party, and vice versa. On the other hand, some men in the confidence of the opposing political party in government had to be admitted to every ministry. This so called "proportional system" was very unpopular but could not be removed during this period. In 1966, for the first time since World War II, Austria had a one-party government (the People's Party), a situation that occurred again in 1970 with the Socialist Party. A mono-coloured government has posed serious problems for ministers who take over a position that was previously held by the opposite party for a long period. It is true that the principle of strict neutrality has been emphasized in public employment ever since 1966, but it refers to impartiality when administering law. The real question raised in such situations, however, is how to set new goals since some ministries have become bastions of one political party. The senior officials, of course, have not refused to cooperate with a new Minister from the other party, but it became obvious that they could not be expected to draft a new policy that reflected his particular political stance.

Attempts to solve this problem have taken two directions: Some preparatory work has been taken away from the ministry and is done in the offices of pressure groups or the party machine, and the new minister has tried to hire men of his own party. However, each civil servant is appointed to a certain job and can be removed without his consent only on serious grounds. This has become a problem as far as the highest civil service positions are concerned. A number of senior officials have retired and a minister's political partisans have been promoted to those jobs. However, no solution can be applied generally. It appears that a minister's only alternative is to ignore the fixed job hierarchy and bring in a political colleague from the outside as his secretary. Staffs view this method with alarm because leading officials have now been subordinated to young outsiders and have had, in practice, to give up some of their functions. The system fails to provide for the integration of political necessity and the traditional status of public employees, and there is little inclination in Austria to settle this problem as it has been settled, for instance, in Germany. In Germany, jobs for so-called political employees have been created, and applicants are aware that they may be released if the government changes. However, public employees seem to object to the introduction of this institution in Austria in the same way that they object to the present practice of installing secretaries to the Minister. If governments change in the future, and this presumption must be fundamental in every democracy, the underlying problem must be solved in one way or the other.

Feasible future developments

We must be prepared for a continued growth of the number of public employees since this reflects increasing tasks of the state. From 1966 to 1970, the Austrian government tried to reduce the number of public employees by decreasing the number of planned jobs and restricting hiring, but this policy has proven to be unsuccessful. A gap has always existed between the number of planned jobs and the number of actual appointments, and to a certain degree this policy has been effective in minimizing the gap although it has also caused an increased demand for new hiring that cannot be ignored any longer.

It is not too farfetched, however, to forecast structural changes. The number of positions for lawyers will be reduced in the public service, and more jobs will become available for social scientists. Nevertheless, the number of positions held by lawyers will probably remain higher than in other countries since the Austrian administration will continue to have a strong legal orientation in the future. There is no doubt that the established institutions of the Constitutional Court and the Administrative Court will continue to control the administration according to traditional rules and principles.

Another problem will be how to stimulate productivity in the sector of public administration. The present wage structure treats individual working performance in a rather indirect way and rigidly relates wages to seniority rather than to performance. Job performance at the present time is stimulated by other means. Special attempts have been made to improve the system of additional allowances and there is always the inducement of early promotion. There is no legal obstacle to promotion even if somebody is hired over the head of a senior official. However, even in an unusual case where a young man is promoted in one step to the highest job available, his wages, at best, will remain lower for a long time since wages are related to seniority rather than to the job. The principle of seniority, still in practice today, was originally introduced to guarantee some independence for public employees. In the past the position of public employees had to be strengthened against nepotism while, at present, this protection is supposed to be necessary to weaken political influence. Life employment and seniority will therefore not be abandoned in the near future. However, it will be more necessary in the future to engage experts as contract employees rather than as civil servants because the rigid wage structure for civil servants will not provide for sufficient salaries. For that reason special contracts for contract employees are becoming more important, and this trend may cause a breakdown of the present structure in the future, although nobody can forecast if and when this will occur.

It seems certain that labor law and public service law will continue to develop on equal terms. In my opinion, the differences will become even smaller. Specifically, the extension of industrial safety law into the public sector may be expected during the next years, which is an actual goal of the trade unions representing public employees.

However, the difference between contract employees and civil servants under public law will not disappear. There was a time before the statute concerning civil servants (*Dienstpragmatik,*

1914) was issued when the unions of the contract employees vehemently opposed the distinction because of its presumption of subordinate status for their members. However, when the government granted improved labor conditions to the contract employees, their unions dropped their insistence that the distinction be eliminated.

The vast majority of *Beamte* are nevertheless convinced that the technical distinction between their terms of appointment and those of the contract employees is a source of special status. For example, blue-collar and white-collar employees feel promoted if their jobs are transferred into civil service status even without an increase in wages. Although public employees as a group have lost much of the special reputation they once held, the individual civil servant (*Beamte*) still has social status and prestige which has not been accorded the *Vertragsbedienstete* and which is highly valued by the former. Hence, the legal distinction between the two cannot be expected to be eliminated in the next few years.

Nor are structural changes in collective bargaining likely to take place. Austrian trade unions, unlike those in the Federal Republic of Germany, have not attempted to substitute collective agreements for the present day system of consultation. They are convinced that a formal substitution would not be followed by any substantial advantage for the civil servants. In addition, in spite of their importance in practice, some authors regarded collective agreements as inconsistent with the Constitution. However doubtful this may be, it does seem certain that collective agreements would infringe on the constitutional framework protecting the rights of civil servants. Thus, collective agreements in the public sector might be a means of settling conflicts once present laws governing civil servants have been dropped in favour of a new conception based on civil labour law. Since this is unlikely, we conclude that collective agreements will not be installed in public services.

The question of strikes remains. Since public service law is dependent on general labour law, moderate treatment of public employee strikes cannot be expected unless there are substantial changes in labour law. According to labour law, workers who go on strike without giving sufficient notice commit an infringement of their employment contract and may be fired. The same principle hinders employers from locking out their workers during the period of the employment contracts. Because of this principle a strike by public employees cannot be regarded as a rightful action. However, in practice private employers will not fire strikers nor will striking public servants be dismissed, and labour conflicts are frequently settled by final agreements providing for the protection of strikers. As indicated earlier, strikes in the private or public sectors are not the usual means of settling disputes in modern Austria, and trade unions, in general, vehemently object to the idea of strike legislation. A special plan for strikes in the public sector is therefore not expected.

As already mentioned, the government has not used its substantial stake in the private economy to obtain general compliance for an income and wage policy. Neither has the government tried to influence the general development of wages by special activities in the public service. It has been suggested that the control over nationalized industry should be used to set some standards, especially those regarding fringe benefits, but attempts in this direction have not been effective, and it is doubtful whether the government might try to use the public sector as a model for a wage and income policy in the future. Even if the government should decide on this course of action the highly centralized Austrian Trade Union Confederation is not likely to tolerate any pattern-setting by what it considers marginal unions. Any attempt to realize a wage and income policy in Austria must start with negotiations at the top level between the government, the Austrian Trade Union Confederation, and the Federal Chamber of Economy. In fact the Joint Commission on Wages and Prices is the permanent body for such discussions. This commission, which has become well-known in Europe, has been set up by these top organizations with government support. The legal basis of the Commission is a gentleman's agreement and, consequently, legally enforceable sanctions have not been available so far, although strong motivation for cooperative activities between the government and these top organizations has developed within this Commission. Thus, we have to assume that any future initiatives for a wage and income policy will come from this Commission and nowhere else.

1. The reviews list all jobs available in the federal service regardless of whether those positions are, in fact, filled or not. The Federal Job Plan for 1973, for example, refers to 150,418 jobs available for civil servants and 129,-529 for contract employees. By way of comparison, the figures for 1965 were 123,117 for civil servants and 150,105 for contract employees. Since, as indicated, there are no data giving the exact number of actual employees, it is doubtful that, for example, the number of contract employees has dropped as sharply as those figures would indicate.

8

Collective Bargaining by Civil Servants in the Nordic Countries

Nils Elvander*

T HE states' role as an employer of its citizens has become
much more important in the Nordic countries** during recent decades. The number of civil servants has increased greatly;
their labor unions have become more powerful and, to a great
extent, as a result of this development, they have obtained the
right to negotiate collective contracts according to rules similar
to those applied to negotiations in the private sector.

The rights of Swedish civil servants to negotiate is relatively
well reviewed in literature.[1] However, except for some articles
in periodicals, there are no published accounts of collective bargaining in Norway, Denmark, and Finland. Therefore, the following comparative description and analysis is based to a large
degree on legal writings, labor contracts, and interviews with
representatives of the negotiating parties. It summarizes the
background of civil servants' labor unions, the main features of

* Professor of Political Science, Uppsala University.
＋Iceland
** The Nordic countries are Denmark, Norway, Sweden, and Finland. When
the designation "Scandanavian" is used in this chapter, it refers to the first
three of these countries only.

the bargaining system, and the existing labor rules for the private sector; describes the development of the civil servants' right to negotiate and the extent of adaptation to the rule system of the private sector; and discusses the reasons for the differences that have developed between the four Nordic countries. Finally, it describes and compares some of the main features of the present bargaining system.[2]

The civil servants' labor unions

The civil servants' bargaining system is influenced to some extent by the structure of their labor unions. It can be assumed that the stronger and more centralized a country's civil servants labor unions are, the more extensive are the bargaining rights and the lesser the differences between bargaining rights in the private and public sectors.

Historically, there were two advances in the development of white-collar labor unions in Scandinavia. The first occurred during and after the first world war when groups of civil servants founded national unions. Some unions had been started at the end of the 1800s, but reductions in real wages during the inflationary war years produced a bond of professional consciousness among the public employees. In contrast to the expanding unions of workers in the private sector in Scandinavia, the newly developed principal organizations of public employees became small and weak during the years between the world wars. Although workers in the private sector belatedly became aware of the professional consciousness of the public workers, their rapidly growing unions in the past decade gave the private sector unions the support of the majority of private employees. (They have, however, a long way to go to reach the civil servants unions' high percentage of membership, which in the Nordic countries averages around 80 percent.)

The second development in organizational structure came about at the end of World War II with the appearance of large national labor federations that combined employees in the public and private sectors. The Swedish TCO (*Tjänstemännens Centralorganisation*), the Swedish Central Organization of Salaried

Employees, was founded in 1944 through the merger of two older central unions. A counterpart organization, the *Tjanstemannaorganisationeras Centralförbund* (TOC) was created in Finland the same year; in Norway the *Funksjonaerernes Sentralorganisasjon* was started in 1951, and in Denmark was founded in 1952. The Norwegian federation never had more than about 25,000 members and was terminated in the beginning of the 1960s. Sweden's role as "the leading country"—a role that has its natural explanation in the fact that the country was spared from the war—became even more apparent when professional groups began to organize at the same time. SACO *(Sveriges Akademikers Centralorganisätion)*, the Swedish federation of professional employees started in 1947, obtained counterparts in the neighboring countries in 1950, and all of these professional federations are still in existence today. In addition, for a long time large white-collar groups have been connected with their respective blue-collar union federation in all the Nordic countries. In Sweden, these groups belong to the *Landsorganisation* or LO. Relatively speaking, the Norweigian *Statstjenstemannskartellet* is the largest of these combined federations.

The modern Swedish labor structure is the most centralized and firmly unified of those in Scandinavia and, to some extent, has provided an example for the neighboring countries. The TCO is the largest of the three main white-collar federations that exist; membership at the end of 1972 was 805,000, compared with the LO's 1,772,000. TCO is a relatively loosely organized federation without its own right to negotiate. The 20 national unions are grouped into three sectors—a public sector group called the TCO-S, which negotiates with public employers, a local government organization TCO-K, whose member unions still negotiate separately for the local employees, and lastly, a sector for employees in private industry. In recent years the private sector group has developed a tendency to negotiate cooperatively with certain SACO unions.

The cooperation between some TCO and SACO unions—which has recently obtained a more limited counterpart in the local government sector—is a remarkable phenomenon in contrast to the early tense relations between the two groups. Among other things the antagonisms have touched on varying philosophies of unionism. While the TCO supports the concept of vertical organization of all white-collar employees, SACO is founded on the horizontal principle (organization according to university degrees). But since reforms in the educational system tend to break up older academic rigidities, SACO's union principles appear today as somewhat old-fashioned. The SACO leadership is attempting to expand its recruitment. Membership is over 120,000, and it is likely to continue to grow. SACO will obtain a large addition in 1975 (16,000 new members) through a merger with *Statstjänstemannens Riksforbund* (SR), the third existing federation of white-collar employees. SR was founded in 1946, although predecessor organizations had existed since 1917. The union is set up horizontally and recruits certain groups of civil servants in the higher salary grades. But because of its small size, SR has found it relatively difficult to manage on its own in connection with negotiations and, therefore, has closely cooperated with the SACO during the last years. (Both organizations now have negotiation rights with the state.) After the merger SACO will go through a drastic efficiency improvement: Thirty unions will be combined with five large organizations.

Finland's employee unions are like Sweden's in many ways. There are three main unions: *Tjanstemannaorganisationeras Centralförbund* (TOC) is the largest with 260,000 members. (The Finnish LO membership is 760,000.) TOC's background dates back to 1922, while the two main organizations, which together founded the Swedish TCO, originated in the 1930s. TOC has the same structure as TCO. The unions as a rule are built up vertically. In the public sector there is a common negotiating organization TCO-T, in which even local government employees are included. As in Sweden, the private employee unions have separate contracts, but a coordinating delegation for negotiations exists.

Supervisors do not belong to TOC but, in general, are members of *Finlands Tekniska Funktionärorganisationers Centralförbund* (FTFC). With over 40,000 members, it is the third largest of the main Finnish unions. Most of its members are privately employed. FTFC was founded in 1946 and is built upon horizontal professional union lines. The same holds true for the *Akademikernas Centralorganisation*, which, when the name is shortened in Finnish, is called *Akava*. Like SACO, *Akava* is attempting to expand recruitment, having even removed the concept of restricting membership to academics. *Akava's* more than 50,000 members are, for the most part, employed in the public sector, and for these *Akava* has complete negotiation rights, which is not the case among its members who work in the private sector. Its present relationship to the TOC is characterized by competition and fringe quarrels.

As was noted earlier, Norway no longer has any central federation for white-collar employees in public and private positions. The reasons why the Norwegian white-collar employee federation failed is not clear, but information from interviews and the data from the remaining employee unions provide certain clues. One explanation seems to be that ever since the 1930s the *Statstjenstemannskartellet* (Cartel) within LO has been a strong union with negotiation rights and with ambitions to recruit even public employees in the highest salary grades. With over 90,000 members, the Cartel is today the largest public employee union in Norway. This can be said to correspond with Sweden's LO-associated unions of white-collar workers such as *Statsanstalldas Forbund* and also the greater part of TCO-S, the main public employment group. With such power within its own control, it was tempting for the Norwegian LO to attempt to recruit still larger employee groups, even in the private sector. Consequently, the LO in Norway opposed the new white-collar employee federation during the 50s. It did not want a large, politically neutral competitive federation. Unfortunately, the other independent public employee unions refused to give up their independent negotiation rights by combining into a cooperative federation. The most important of these unions is *Norsk Laererlag* (with about 30,000 members), which most nearly corresponds with the TCO-associated union *Sveriges Lärarförbund* (Swedish Teachers Union), but also recruits principals and many lectors. Just as in Sweden and Finland, there are plans for a single Norwegian teachers union, but the lectors in the Civil Service Federation *Embetsmennenes Landsforbund* (EL) have opposed these plans. EL, with over 20,000 members, is the next largest of the independent public employee unions. The union, which was founded in 1918, has a horizontal structure. This has made cooperation with *Norges Akademikersamband* (NAS) a natural thing since many of its members also hold membership in NAS. (About 40 percent of the 35,000 NAS members are state employed, with EL as their negotiating organization.) In 1960, EL became an independent part of the NAS, but because of various differences the two organizations split in 1968. Now, however, they plan to cooperate again—a "Norwegian SACO" is their goal. For the sake of completeness it should also be noted that there exist two additional independent unions for public employees in Norway. The most important is STAFO, which is just as large as the EL and recruits mostly office workers.

The Danish counterpart to TCO is the *Faellesrodet for Danske Tjenestemands-og Funktionaerorganistioner* (FTF). It was founded in 1952, and now has about 230,000 members (compared to the Danish LO's 924,000). Like the TCO, the FTF has no negotiating rights. The biggest difference between them is that the Danish federation is a conglomerate of many unions and small associations whose negotiations on behalf of public employees are handled by certain component unions rather than by FTF's "sections." FTF has a common influence on governmental wage policy and can give the member unions help with negotiations, but there exists no counterpart to Sweden's TCO-S and Finland's TOC-T. The largest FTF union is *Danmarks Laererforening,* which mainly organizes public school teachers and negotiates with the state. As a rule the private employee groups in FTF participate in separate negotiation. Danish supervisors and officials, as in Finland, have their own main organization.

In its beginnings, from 1950, the Danish professional movement was loosely united, but during the last years it has been consolidated. It has also incorporated a part of the early FTF-associated professional groups and in this way has become more like SACO. In 1972, the name was changed to *Akademikernas Centralorganisation* (AC). Membership is now over 60,000. AC has bargaining rights for about 10,000 public employees (*tjenestemaend*).

Besides the teachers' union and the AC there are two additional main bargaining units for the Danish state's *tjenstemaend*. They were established in the beginning of the 20th century and are called quite simply *Centralorganisation I* (CO I) and *Centralorganisation II* (CO II). The difference between CO I, which mainly includes lower ranked public employees, and CO II, higher ranked civil servants, reflects presumed status distinctions carried over from the 19th century. The employees in CO I belong simultaneously to different unions within LO and FTF, while CO II in its entirety belongs to FTF. What has been said to this point concerns only actual civil servants to whom special pensions and employment circumstances apply. It should be pointed out that they are denied the right to strike. This group's negotiations are handled therefore by CO I, CO II, *Laererforeningen* (Teachers' Association) and, to a small extent, by AC. *Tjenstemaendenes Faellesudvalg* (TFU) coordinates negotiations of these four organizations and bargains for general wages and working conditions with the government. The main portion of the remaining public employees have their employment conditions determined through collective bargaining (*overenskomstansatte*), which means that they are appointed on a group contract basis under the private employment rules. Therefore they have the right to strike. Manual workers and many professional employees belong in this category for which AC exercises de facto negotiating rights. This complicated organizational setup of the public sector in Denmark can be shown somewhat more clearly by the diagram below.

The organizational structure in the public sector is more splintered in Norway and Denmark than it is in Sweden and Finland. In Norway there is no counterpart to the strong negotiating bodies outside the LO-territory, as in Sweden and Finland (the TCO-S and TOC-T respectively). In Denmark TFU exercises considerable power over its associated unions in connection with negotiations, but, on the other hand, the organization's structure is complicated through the separation of civil servants into *tjenestemaend* and *overenskomstansatte*. The principle of horizontal professional unionism is more dominant in Norway and Denmark than it is in the neighboring countries and, as a result, the authority of the central unions over member unions is limited.

Organization of the public sector in Denmark

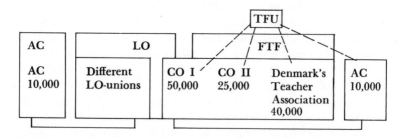

<table>
<tr><td></td><td></td><td></td><td>TFU</td><td></td><td></td></tr>
</table>

Overenskomstansatte
(total 60,000)
(Collective bargaining &
right to strike)

Civil Servants
(125,000 belong of a total of 135,000)
(Limited negotiations without
right to strike.)

The negotiating system in the private sector

Around the turn of the century, collective bargaining between the national labor unions and the corresponding employer organizations began in Scandinavia. Modern negotiating forms and more peaceful legal relations developed first in Denmark since industrialization occurred much earlier in Denmark than in the other Nordic countries and by the 1880s Denmark's Social Democratic Party had chosen a more moderate reform strategy. In contrast, the development of collective bargaining in Finland was delayed not only by late industrialization but also by severe political conflict. Finland's civil war of 1918 resulted in social and political reverberations, which are felt even to this day. Collective bargaining came to the Finnish labor market after the second world war. Even then, labor unrest has been much more intense in Finland than in the neighboring countries, in part because of communism's strong standing and the political splintering within the national labor unions.

Differences in the rate of development of collective bargaining between the four Nordic countries can be illustrated by the varying points in time when the so-called basic agreements came into effect. These deal with rules for negotiations, strike rights, etc. The basic agreement was agreed to between the LO and the employer organizations in Denmark in 1899, Norway in 1935, Sweden in 1938, and Finland in 1944. Norway and Sweden took an intermediate position. This position also influenced the time when a centralized system of negotiations was developed on the national level. In Denmark, central negotiations on two-year agreements between LO and the employers organization came about in the mid-1930s. The corresponding change in Sweden occurred in the middle of the 1950s, and in Norway not until the beginning of the 1960s. However, in Finland resistance to centralized negotiations has been so strong within certain unions (especially those that are communist-dominated) that the centralized system, built up with difficulty during the 1960s, collapsed in 1973.

A characteristic feature of Nordic collective bargaining systems is the distinction between rights disputes and interest disputes. By *rights disputes* is meant disputes about interpretation of existing collective bargaining agreements and working rules. Such disputes are not allowed to result in strikes but must be settled in a peaceful manner through negotiations and, as a last resort, through labor courts. An *interest dispute* refers to disagreements over different desired ends, over issues not yet agreed upon, or issues that are regulated through legislation or bargaining. A typical interest dispute arises over negotiations on new collective agreements or prolongation of an earlier agreement. On such a disagreement, the parties have the right to take offensive action—strikes or lockouts—provided that the old agreement has expired. Prior to that time they are subject to a co-called "peace obligation."

The main distinction between rights disputes and interest disputes is the peace obligation during the life of the agreement. This obligation, which is less common in the rest of Europe, has strong benefits for peaceful labor relations. This is the case with Scandinavian countries where legislation is complemented by rules in the basic agreement on limitations of strike rights, separate negotiations for local rights disputes, and rules for settlement of interest disputes. However, in Finland the peace obligation is not as binding as in the neighboring countries because it does not apply to individual workers. Workers, therefore, cannot be condemned individually by the labor court for participation in illegal strikes. The frequency of wildcat strikes is much higher in Finland than in the three Scandinavian countries.

One result of the distinction between rights and interest disputes has been that special government labor courts have been established for the handling of rights disputes that cannot be resolved through bargaining. In Denmark this came about through legislation in 1910. (A voluntary predecessor was set up by the parties themselves in 1899 through the first basic agreement.) Similar legislation was enacted in Norway in 1915, in Sweden in 1928, and in Finland not until 1946. The labor courts have similar structure and tasks in all the Nordic countries. They are made up of neutrals (legally trained judges, of whom one is chairman) and of members who are nominated (except in Denmark) by the parties and appointed by the government with equal representation from each side. One result of the government civil servants and local civil servants having obtained negotiation rights is that, in recent years, representatives of the public employee unions and the public employers have obtained places in the labor court. These representatives replace the representatives of the private sector in lawsuits that concern rights disputes in the public sector.

The Danish labor court holds a unique position in two respects. Its jurisdiction is limited to breaches of the basic agreement and collective contracts and the parties themselves rather than the government select their representatives in the court. Interpretation disputes, which in the other Nordic countries are settled as a last resort by the labor court, are resolved according to special rules of mediation and arbitration under the parties' own agreement. The peculiar and unique method of selecting the members of the court (who in turn select the chairman)— giving the labor court in Denmark less of the character of a state organ than in the other Nordic countries—has historical reasons. As already mentioned, the parties' own first basic agreement in 1899 was a predecessor to the Danish labor court. It had the character of an arbitration court with the function of settling disputes dealing with alleged violations of the basic agreement. This system has remained largely unchanged to this day. It is a symbol of a system of rules created mainly by the parties. It typifies a lasting tradition in Denmark where labor law rules appear to a greater extent than in neighboring countries to be created by labor unions and agreed to by employers. Thus, Denmark lacks special legislation concerning collective agreements, while in Norway and Sweden such laws were established at the same time that the labor court was founded. (In Finland, a law concerning collective agreements was passed in 1924, but did not have any practical impact due to employer opposition.)

In interest disputes the Nordic states normally intervene only through regularized procedures for mediation. In Denmark and Norway the national mediators have wide-reaching authority, especially concerning the right to postpone the beginning of strike action. They also have the option to push through collective solutions of conflicts that affect several unions. This is done in such a way that minority groups are often voted down in combined membership votes on proposed settlements. Voting on proposals for contract agreements and proposed mediation settlements plays a big part in the labor movement in Denmark and especially in Norway. Combined with the splintered union organizational structure, especially in the public civil servants sector, mediator control of voting has created troubling moments for the labor movement. It could almost be said that mediation in Denmark and Norway has become a weapon against splintering and small unions.

The Swedish model is one of representative democracy in

strong, centralized unions that stand against all forms of public intervention and take full responsibility for the preservation of labor peace. This is the reason why, compared with the neighboring countries, the institution of mediation in Sweden has little formal authority. The parties have chosen not to have a strong mediation institution of the Danish-Norwegian type and, through a practical move to eliminate membership strike votes that were the rule during the union movements' founding around the turn of the century, they have been able to demonstrate that the practice of "strong" mediation is not needed. In contrast to its neighboring countries, Sweden does not have a permanent "National Mediator" but only regional mediators who have no authority to prevent or suspend strikes. In recent years, a new provision has been added in the mediation law, however, which gives the government the right to call a special mediation commission. This is a consequence of the central negotiation system. Repeatedly since 1964, the Swedish mediation commissioners have met to try to unify the parties in the central negotiations in the private sector. Since 1966, these same efforts have also taken place in the public sector.

Finland takes an intermediate position between Denmark, Norway, and Sweden concerning the authority of the mediation institution. Government intervention has increased little by little, probably as a result of constant unrest in the labor market. For the present there are three government mediators, one of whom is concerned with mediating conflicts in the public sector. They have about the same authority to work out delays in strikes as their counterparts in Denmark and Norway. On the other hand, there is no equivalent to the Danish-Norwegian rules controlling voting on mediation proposals, perhaps because membership voting generally plays a smaller role in Finland. The one exception is in those unions that are controlled by the communists, where strike votes are more common.

In special cases in Nordic countries, the state can also intervene in interest disputes in a more active way than through mediation. The state can exercise power in situations where the public interest is threatened by open industrial conflict. This power has been exercised in the different countries to different extents and with different methods, either continuous intervention according to fixed rules or, more rarely, with ad hoc decisions. A typical example of the former methods is the Norwegian system of compulsory arbitration. Denmark has a long-standing tradition of government intervention in crisis situations, although without hard and fast rules. In Sweden and Finland, compulsory intervention is rare and the so-called doctrine of the free labor market is upheld most consistently in Sweden. In summary, Norway and Denmark have a long tradition of state intervention in negotiating impasses; Finland takes an intermediate position, and Sweden intervenes least of all.

In Denmark the government has intervened twenty-odd times since 1933, by legislating on labor conflicts in the private sector. As a rule the Social Democratic government intervenes in this way to help the trade union movement, usually in the way of legislation on the basis of a mediation proposal. Some indications suggest, however, that the government and the parties now wish to eliminate the intervention system. In 1973 the government allowed a large conflict to break out between the LO and the employers' organization without intervention. The strike lasted only a short time since a renewed attempt at negotiations led to an agreement.

The idea of compulsory arbitration has always been fundamentally opposed by the parties in Denmark, Sweden, and Finland. Although the same holds true for Norway, this has not prevented compulsory arbitration from becoming something of a permanent institution in that country. In the beginning, binding arbitration of interest disputes was implemented only as a temporary, limited arrangement during the first world war but the arbitration law was extended to 1921 and re-established twice during the 1920s. As in the neighboring countries, it was chiefly the Norwegian Liberal Party that supported compulsory arbitration. The Liberals succeeded in getting their way because at the time they held a stronger position in Norway than in other Nordic countries. During that period there was greater unrest in the Norwegian labor market partly because the Norwegian labor movement developed in a very radical, almost syndicalistic direction. During the 1930s, when the Social Democrats became a reformist government party, which it had been long before in Denmark and Sweden, no compulsory arbitration took place. However, in 1945, the Social Democratic government reinstituted arbitration in agreement with the LO and the employer organizations. Although compulsory arbitration was thought of as a temporary means to facilitate the country's reconstruction after the war, it became a permanent measure.

Now, in accordance with the existing law of 1952, arbitration is normally used on a voluntary basis in Norway and is instituted on the request of both parties to a permanent National Arbitration Board. This Board has a structure like that of the labor court. But it is also understood that the government and the parliament have the legislative right in every special case to submit an interest dispute case to the Arbitration Board, which is in effect compulsory binding arbitration. This has occurred about 40 times since 1952. Compulsory arbitration has often been used to prevent large, nation-wide conflicts, even in the public sector, while voluntary arbitration usually applies to small, local disputes and has been used somewhat less. The high incidence of compulsory arbitration and the great power of the national mediation officials can be attributed to union splintering and the power of the voting institution in Norway.

In Sweden, compulsory intervention legislation has been prepared at three different times since the second world war but was never put into effect since the disputes were solved before enactment became necessary. In two of these cases, the disputes concerned workers in the local government sector. When civil servants and local employees obtained complete negotiation and strike rights in 1965, the idea of an emergency law was discussed. This would have provided general guidelines for dispute intervention in conflicts that would affect and endanger the community. But the government rejected this idea and decided that the parties should be allowed to take the responsibility for avoiding such conflicts. In the private sector the basic agreement was reached in 1938, by which the parties agreed to avoid stoppages endangering the public. With this as a model, two basic agreements for public employees were developed, one for the national sector and one for the local, which stated that questions concerning conflicts that would endanger the community should be dealt with according to certain rules decided on by the negotiating parties.

The first, and thus far the only, complete instance of dispute intervention in Sweden occurred in the spring of 1971 in the public sector. Opposition to the national and local authorities' wage equalization policy led to SACO and SR proclaiming several strikes, which the employers responded to with widespread lockouts. The government and parliament passed a law that extended collective contracts for six weeks, during which time strikes were forbidden. Later on a new agreement was peacefully concluded between the parties.

Finland has provided for wage regulation and strike control through so-called "emergency legislation" during two periods. The first period occurred while wage regulation was in effect during the second world war and for the following ten years. In practice, however, the wage controls were not very effective and the prohibition of strikes could not be enforced after the war. Governmental powers were initiated once again at the close of the 1960s as one part in the income policy that was beginning to be put into effect according to the so-called "stabilization agreement" between the government, the unions, and the employer organizations. The wage regulating power never needed to be used, however, since the parties could make agreements within the limits of the general wage restraint policy. In general it can be said that the state in Finland has had greater formal powers to intervene in wage establishment than in Sweden, but that, in practice, freedom of the labor market has been greater in Finland since dispute intervention has not taken place. This is equally true of the public sector. When Finnish state and local civil servants obtained the right to strike in 1970, it was expected that a law prohibiting strikes detrimental to the public good would be quickly passed, but up to the present this has not been necessary.

The state as employer

In Norway and Denmark large groups of civil servants obtained negotiation rights and the right to strike much earlier than similar groups in Sweden and Finland. But, on the other hand, the right to strike has been extended more widely in the latter two countries. Certain categories of civil servants in Norway and Denmark have no right to strike, while such limitations exist relatively less often in Sweden and Finland.

These developments came about earlier in Norway. The Civil Servants Act (*tjenstemannsloven*) of 1918 did not guarantee bargaining rights but it did indirectly recognize one type of strike right—the right to cancel an agreement—for all civil servants except the so-called "irremovable" civil servants at the highest level. The next step occurred in 1933, when a law concerning bargaining rights was passed as a part of a wage agreement. The state still retained the formal right to decide on an issue, however. This was further changed by the Civil Service Disputes Act of 1958 (*tjenstetvistloven*). The system now legalized collective bargaining (*tariffavtaler*) and also recognized the reciprocal peace obligation during the contract period that had developed in practice during the years after the war. The existing private sector rules concerning mediation, arbitration, and the labor court became applicable to civil servants. When this act was revised in 1969, the most important change was that the states' right to answer strikes with lockouts was clearly set forth. In practice, about 5,000 Norwegian civil servants as well as all army and police officers and patrolmen, are denied the right to strike.[3]

In Denmark, as mentioned earlier, there is a division between *tjenestemaend* and *overenskomstansatte,* which is of fundamental importance. The *overenskomstansatte* (collectively employed) obtained generally complete negotiation and strike rights during the 1930s. Professional groups have pressed for many years to obtain the same free collective bargaining rights. They finally obtained the right to strike in 1971 as a result of negotiations between the state and their professional main unions. At the state level after the second world war, the *tjenestemaend* obtained a real right to negotiate wages and terms of employment. This negotiation right was codified in 1969 through a *tjenestemaendslov* and a basic agreement between the state and the four central organizations. But the right to strike has never been granted to this large group, about 135,000, of state employees. The *tjenestemaend* also remain outside the rule system that applies to private sector employees and *overenskomstansatte*. For example, all civil service rights disputes for this category are handled by a special *Voldgiftsret i tjenestemandssager,* established separately in 1919.[4]

Developments in Sweden and Finland resemble those of Norway and Denmark in that a collective bargaining system developed in practice before being enacted into law. However, when legal enactment took place in the latter two countries, no limitations were placed on many public employees' right to strike. In Sweden, the civil servants obtained negotiation rights in 1937, but they were extremely limited and the state retained final decision-making power. Civil service negotiation rights developed after the war into a central, periodic negotiation system between equal parties. As in the neighboring countries, these negotiations became coordinated with the central negotiations in the private sector. Government and parliament approval of the negotiated agreements became more and more a formality. The unions desired complete negotiation rights and a switch to the private sector rule system for state and local workers. This goal was achieved through a parliamentary decision of 1965, which went into effect on January 1, 1966, the same time as basic agreements between the unions and the public employers became effective.[5]

In Finland, the civil servants were given limited negotiation rights through a law passed in 1943, which resembled the Swedish Act of 1937. Through the so-called procedure law, which was in effect from 1966-70, a contract system was instituted with yearly adjustment of wages. But still the state retained the final right of decision. At the time of the Stabliization Agreement of 1968, the employee aim of obtaining complete negotiation rights was again brought up. The result was that the laws were revised to give state and local civil servants collective bargaining and strike rights in 1970. As in Sweden, the negotiating process is regulated by basic agreements to deal with conflicts that could be dangerous to the society. The Finnish civil servants accepted the rules concerning intervention that apply generally in Sweden. At the same time that this was accepted, a second national mediator was introduced and the rules on mediation and the labor court were extended to public sector disputes.[6]

In the author's opinion, the right to strike should be thought of as an essential element of a free bargaining system. Practically all public employees have this right in Sweden and Finland. Why were some groups of civil servants in Denmark and Norway given the right to strike very early while other groups are still denied it? The answer seems to lie in different administrative traditions. Denmark is characterized by a more "continental" administrative tradition with its roots in the divine right of kings and absolutist state power. This tradition colors public employer and employee outlook on the obligation of government service and still has a strong hold on their attitudes, stronger than in the neighboring countries. But it only applies to permanent civil service employees, the state's *tjenstemaend*. Other public workers were permitted to have collective bargaining systems as early as the years beween the wars.

As a result of its connection to Denmark before 1814, Norway has been influenced by the Danish administrative traditions, which may explain why it is generally accepted that some civil servants are not allowed the right to strike.[7] But, on the other hand, the great majority of Norwegian civil servants received complete negotiation rights and strike rights earlier than in any of the neighboring countries (1958). Perhaps this can be seen as a response to the strong democratic spirit in Norway, which is evident in many areas of the society as well as in the labor market. It is enlightening that an attempt in the 1920s to forbid civil servant strikes failed because of union opposition. During the preparatory work for the 1958 legislation, the Norwegian government announced that it would be outrageous if the right to strike which had in fact existed since 1918, should be limited.[8]

In Sweden, the traditional independence of the administrative agencies and their personnel, separating them from the government departments, has been one reason why a public law outlook was so completely replaced by rules and norms from the private sector when the great reform was decided in 1965. As in

Norway, the greatest stumbling block in earlier reform attempts had been the view that the concept of "irremovability" of higher civil servants was incompatible with the right to strike. The question was solved by transferring one of the labor court's traditional principles—that conflict does not vacate a position—from the private to the public sector. In Finland, the 1970 laws, like much of its other public labor legislation, are linked to the Swedish developments because Finnish organizational and administrative traditions correspond more with Sweden than with Denmark and Norway.

Present variations in the right to strike can also be explained by union attitudes. Swedish and Finnish unions desired that no restrictions on the right to strike be enacted and, in general, this became the states' decision. In Sweden, however, the great SACO-SR conflict in 1971 caused the introduction of some new restrictions in a new basic agreement, which was concluded by the state and the unions in 1973 (the old agreement was cancelled by SACO). The parties agreed that the right to take strike action "ought to be used with great caution" to protect important societal functions. Certain staff groups in leading positions in the judicial, medical, religious, and educational systems; all the chiefs of the central administrative authorities, and all workers within the state departments were excluded from the right to strike. In all, this limitation affects about 8,000 people. (At the start of the new negotiation systems in 1966, only about 450 people in head positions had been excluded through an agreement with the unions.) [9] This is a substantial number of upper-ranked civil servants who are forbidden to strike in Sweden, but in proportion to the population and work force and the size of the group comparable in Norway, it is relatively small.

In Norway and Denmark the organizations comparable to those mentioned above have not been very interested in the right to strike. This is especially evident in Denmark where the *tjenestemaendenes* unions state that they prefer the prevailing system to the Swedish one, which is looked upon with great scepticism. They believe that the right to strike does not guarantee better negotiating results and might lead to impaired employment security.

Some current problems

Space does not permit a detailed survey of contemporary developments in the public employee bargaining system in the Nordic countries. Instead, this study will conclude with some brief comparative observations concerning three main problems: the contracting parties, exemptions from the scope of bargaining, and rules for the avoidance of conflicts that endanger the society.

In all the Scandinavian countries, the contracting parties on the *employee side* are the civil service federations. In Norway this has been established in the Civil Service Disputes Act through which minimal rules on membership numbers, which are required as a condition for the right to bargain, have been set up. These rules, designed to exclude small groups from the central agreements, should be seen against a background of severe union splintering among salaried employees. In the other countries the union picture is more stable. In these countries the main unions' right to negotiations is not authorized by law; they simply acquire their status through the basic contracts that they have made with the state.

On the *employers side,* the bargaining party is a government department in all the countries except Sweden. Negotiations are conducted by one division or a subordinate organ within the respective departments of state. This system was also used in Sweden before the complete negotiation rights system was put into effect. But in 1965, an independent civil service agency was established, *Statens Avtalsverk* (SAV), which took over the earlier government department's role as the employer. It was thought unfitting for the government as such to take sides when the public employee unions and the component agencies of government obtained the right to take strike and lockout actions. This issue arose again in connection with a conflict within the education sector in 1966, in which SACO's selective strikes were met by the SAV with widespread lockouts. Criticism was directed toward the unclarified locus of responsibility on the employer's side. Government wage policy was said to have led to the strike and to have made SAV's independent negotiating position a fiction. No change in the system has been made, however. But this set of problems concerning the negotiating agency's position is one major reason why not much thought has been given to instituting the Swedish system in the neighboring countries.

In all the Nordic countries, the government must approve the contract and the contracts must be submitted to the respective parliaments in one form or another. In Sweden since 1966, the Parliament's right of decision has been delegated to a Parliamentary wage delegation, which also must be kept informed of the progress of negotiations. Finland instituted the same system in 1970. Denmark has special rules for arriving at a decision if the parties cannot come to an agreement on wages for the *tjenestemaend*. In an impasse, the state decides unilaterally by legislation. If the dispute concerns wage distribution, however, there shall first be secured a statement from *Statens lønningsrad,* an organ of political mediation consisting of representatives of the political parties, the unions, and the government. *Lønningsradet* shall even be consulted concerning dispute questions other than wages, for example, hours of work, but even in these cases, it is ultimately the minister who decides.

Provisions corresponding to the private employer's traditional right to supervise and assign jobs and to hire and dismiss personnel are found in the civil service laws in Sweden and Denmark and in the Civil Service Collective Contract Law (*tjänstekollektivavtalslagen*) in Finland. These laws limit the scope of negotiable issues. The unions in each country, nevertheless, have the right to carry on "discussions" with the states' representatives concerning these matters even though they are not appropriate for inclusion in the contract. In Denmark, this right is codified in the Civil Service Law (*tjenestemandsloven*) (48). In Norway, there is no specific law on these matters, but it is understood that contractual agreements cannot be reached on supervision of civil service jobs and so on.[10]

In Sweden, the boundary between issues negotiable in the contract and those for "discussion" only was one of the most disputed questions when the new bargaining system was instituted. The unions wanted more matters to be covered by contract than the state authorities felt they could agree to. Since then, certain

Country	Unions	Government Department and Component Negotiating Unit
Denmark	TFU, CO I, CO II, AC, *Danmarks Laererforening*	Economy and Budget Department (Wage & Pension Department)
Norway	*Statstjenstemanns-kartellet*, STAFO, EL, YH*, *Norsk Larerlag*	Consumer and Administrative Department (Personnel directorate)
Sweden	*Statsanställdas förbund*, SR, SACO, TCO-S	The States Contract Department
Finland	VTY** *Akava*, TOC-T	Finance Department (The labor market institution)

*YH = The occupational union *Hovedsammenslutning* (a small federation for the military and police, among others).

**VTY = A government employee federation within the Finnish LO.

shifting in the direction of union desires has taken place. In order to comply with worker demands for co-determination over working conditions, the government has recently presented a proposed new formulation of the civil servants' law's "supervision of work" paragraph. The proposed resolution implies that agreements can be made concerning assignment and supervision of work. The only limit set forth is that the contract cannot be allowed to intrude on the states' right to determine the "business" of government authorities and how it should be run.

Rules for the avoidance of civil servant conflicts which would be dangerous to the community have different formulations in the respective countries. In each country they are related to the system for conflict resolution in the private sector. In Norway, this function is given to the National Arbitration Board for arbitration of interest disputes of a general nature. The parties themselves can agree to bring the dispute before the Board (voluntary arbitration), or the government and parliament can pass a law mandating compulsory arbitration. The latter power is used over conflicts that will endanger the community. For disputes on special questions, such as assignment of salary grades, there is a special arbitration commission, called *Statens lønnsutvalg* (The States Wage Committee), which consists of representatives of each party plus three neutral members chosen by the National Mediator. In contrast to cases involving voluntary arbitration, the Wage Committee can intervene at the request of one party only. This is, therefore, a type of compulsory arbitration. This system discourages disputes on wage classifications from developing into major conflicts that could threaten the public interest.[11]

In Denmark, there is no need for rules dealing with conflicts concerning the *tjenestemaend* that threaten the public welfare since these state employees are denied the right to strike. With regard to *overenskomstomradet*, the state, as in the private sector, may intervene through special legislation.

In Sweden and Finland, rules have been made for the prevention of conflicts that threaten the public welfare, but these countries have chosen a different approach than the Norwegian one of compulsory arbitration. According to the Swedish basic agreement, the parties shall mutually appoint a commission, which, on the request of one of the parties, shall decide whether or not the potential conflict will endanger the public. However, this shall not be done until negotiations have been given enough time to achieve a possible peaceful settlement. If negotiations are unsuccessful, and if the commission later determines that the conflict is dangerous to the public welfare, the parties are then asked to avoid conflict. Strikes can be postponed three weeks at the most. But the commission cannot settle a dispute by binding arbitration. To a large extent, Finland adopted the Swedish rules in its collective contract law and basic agreement of 1970, with one important difference. The Finnish commission members are chosen by the National Mediator from among nominees of the parties and he calls the commission together. In both countries the parties agree upon recommendations, but in Finland there is, in effect, neutral participation through the National Mediator's role. This probably results in greater strength in the commission's recommendations in Finland than in Sweden.

1. H. M. Levinson, *Collective Bargaining by Public Employees in Sweden,* (Ann Arbor: Institute of Labor and Industrial Relations, The University of Michigan—Wayne State University, 1972); L. F. Tobisson, *Främvaxten av statstjämst-emamnens forhandlings-rätt* (Stockholm: *Jurist—och Samhällsvetareförbundets Förlag,* 1973) ; N. Elvander, *Intresseorganisationerna i dagens Sverige* (Lund: Gleerup, 1966, second edition, 1969).

2. The following account is based on my essay *"Staten och organisationerna på arbetmarknaden i de nordiska länderna: En komparativ översikt,"* which was published in 1974 in L. Brantgärde, H. Elvander, F. Schmidt, *Konfliktlösning på arbetsmarknaden* (Lund: Gleerup). Part of the essay will be published in 1974 in the *European Journal of Political Research.*

3. B. Döhlen, *"Lov om offentlige tjenestetwister,"* *Nordisk Administrativt Tidskrift* 1959, p. 29; E. S. Lund, *"Utkast til felles lov om embets-og tjenstemenn i Norge,"* *ibid.* 1972, p. 103; Th. Chr. Wyller, *Landsforbund og lønnskamp* (Oslo: Cappelen, 1970), pp. 15, 25, 52.

4. P. Rubak & P. H. Matson, *Tjenestemandslovene m.m.,* second edition (Copenhagen 1972,) pp. 2, 175; A Hastrup, *"Tjenestemandsreformen,"* *Nordisk Administrativt Tidskrift,* 1970, p. 1; H. Lavesen, *"Den danske tjenestemandsreform og efterspillet til denne,"* *ibid.* 1970, p. 18.

5. Elvander, *op. cit.,* (1969), p. 123; Tobisson, *op. cit.,* passim.

6. W. A. Palme, *"Några synpunkter på tjänstemannaorganisationernas förhandlingsrätt,"* *Nordisk Administrativt Tidskrift* 1959, p. 239; O. Tytkölä, *"Lagstiftningen om tjänstemäs förhandlingsrätt och tjänstekollektivavtal,"* *Ibid.* 1972, p. 38.

7. Cf. N. Herlitz, *Nordisk offentlig ratt, III: Regeringsmakt och forvaltningstradition* (Stockholm: Norstedt, 1963), pp. 228, 248, 433, 516.

8. *Proposition till odelstinger nr 20* (1958), p. 21; Wyller, *op. cit.,* p. 25.

9. Basic agreement of April 26, 1973 between *Statens Avtalsverk* and SF, SR, SACO and TCO-S, pp. 6, 13; interview with information chief Bertil Drougge, *Statens Avtalsverk.*

10. This inference is drawn, among other things, from a statement in the proposal to the *tjenestetwistlov* of 1958. Details concerning employment and dismissal, for example, can become subjects for informal consideration.

11. Cf. B. Döhlen, *op. cit., Nordisk Administrativt Tidskrift* 1959, p. 36.

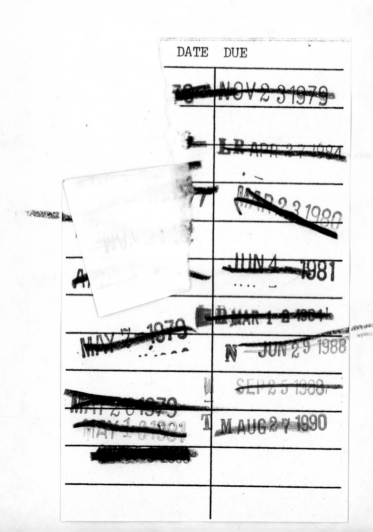